Wreckchasing 102

Exploring military and commercial aircraft crash sites

Nicholas A. Veronico • Ian Abbott • Jeff Christner • Ed Davies • Craig Fuller
David L. McCurry • Michael H. Marlow • Tony Moore • James D. Scroggins III
Scott A. Thompson • David Trojan

In remembrance of the men and women lost in the pursuit of aviation.

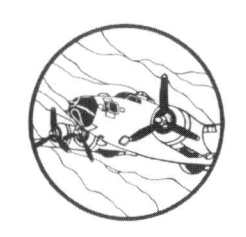

Published by
Pacific Aero Press
P.O. Box 7081
San Carlos, CA 94070

Copyright 2023

Nicholas A. Veronico • Ian Abbott • Jeff Christner • Ed Davies
Craig Fuller • David L. McCurry • Michael H. Marlow • Tony Moore
James D. Scroggins III • Scott A. Thompson • David Trojan

Edited by Beth Hagenauer

Visit the Wreckchasing Message Board at:
www.wreckchasing.com

ISBN: 978-0-9636332-3-1

First Edition • Printed and bound in the United States of America

All rights reserved. No part of this publication may be reproduced, stored in a retrieval system, or transmitted by any means without first seeking written permission of the publisher. The publishers recognizes that certain brand or model names may be copywritten by others and are used here for identification purposes only.

All information contained in this volume is accurate at the time of publication. No guarantee is made to the existence, location, or condition of any aircraft wreck. The pursuit of wreckchasing, hiking, or aircraft salvage can be dangerous. It is the responsibility of the individual and not of the authors or publishers to conduct themselves in a safe manner. Obey all laws and respect the privacy of all landowners where downed aircraft may be located. This volume is presented for informational purposes only.

Front Cover:
B-17C 40-2047 broke up in a storm over California's Sierra Nevada Mountains between Lake Tahoe and Sacramento. The wing section rests inverted on the forest floor as B-17 expert and author Scott A. Thompson inspects the site (Betty Veronico), see page 20. Inset: The crash site of F-100C 54-2090 lies on the face of a remote canyon near Cherry Creek, Nevada (Craig Fuller), see page 118.

Title Page:
A B-24D sits abandoned on the Horanda East 4 airfield at the Dobodura Air Base, Oro Province, New Guinea. Researchers believe this aircraft to be B-24D-150-CO 42-41234, Career Girl, which served with the Fifth Air Force, 380th Bomb Group, 528th Bomb Squadron. (Charles Darby)

Back Cover, left to right:
View of the March 1945, crash of a Navy R4D in San Carlos, California (U.S. Navy photo), see page 68; Airspeed indicator dial face found at the Nevada crash site of P-39Q 44-3586 (James Douglas Scroggins III), see page 32; Nellis AFB Training logo seen on the tail of F-86E 51-12983 as found in the Nevada desert (James Douglas Scroggins III), see page 112.

CONTENTS

Introduction 5

Chapter 1
Washington State's Killer Mountain Claims Three Airliners 6
Ed Davies

Chapter 2
In-Flight Break-up Claims B-17C Flying Fortress 20
Scott Thompson (Nov 1941)

Chapter 3
P-39 Airacobra Gamble: Lost on a Las Vegas Training Mission 32
James D. Scroggins III

Chapter 4
Formation Blunder: B-17 and AT-6 Collide 40
James D. Scroggins III

Chapter 5
Luke Field Missions: A Trio of AT-6s Go Missing 48
Craig Fuller

Chapter 6
Failure at the Factory: Convair Plant Mishaps 56
Nicholas A. Veronico

Chapter 7
Sixteen Survive Navy Transport Crash in San Carlos, California 68
Nicholas A. Veronico and Jeff Christner

Chapter 8
Fist Fight in the Cabin Not a Factor 80
Tony Moore and Nicholas A. Veronico

Chapter 9
Michigan Crash Site Mystery 92
David Trojan

Chapter 10
Searching for Answers at a Beech T-11 Wreck Site. 102
David Trojan

Chapter 11
Air Combat Maneuvering Results in Stall Spin Accident 112
James Douglas Scroggins III

Chapter 12
The Legend of Airplane Canyon 118
David Trojan

Chapter 13
Moffett Field Mid-Air: Collision on Final Approach 130
Ian Abbott

Chapter 14
Paris Departure Disaster: Turkish DC-10 138
Ian Abbott

Chapter 15
Point of No Return: The Crash of American Air Lines Flight 191 Heavy 146
Michael H. Marlow

Chapter 16
Fuel Transfer Stalls Prototype B-1A Bomber 162
David L. McCurry

Bibliography and Suggested Reading 168

About the Authors 174

Introduction

Who wreckchases? Many major aviation museums and private collectors wreckchase. This pursuit of rare aircraft, crashed and forgotten for decades, has brought many types back from extinction.

There are a Junkers Ju 87 dive bomber, a Mitsubishi G4M Betty medium bomber, and a pair of North American F-82 Twin Mustangs under restoration today, and in the case of the XP-82 one of which is now flying, that serve as examples of virtually extinct aircraft types that are making a return from the brink of extinction.

In the early 1970s, restaurateur and businessman David C. Tallichet financed one of the first major wreck recovery efforts. Under the direction of Charles Darby, Tallichet's expedition combed the former airfields of Papua New Guinea and recovered thirty aircraft, nearly tripling the world's P-39 population while rescuing a number of P-40s, an A-20 Havoc twin-engine bomber, as well as a number of rare Bristol Beauforts. A large quantity of Supermarine Spitfires and dozens of Japanese army and navy aircraft wrecks were passed by because Tallichet's collecting efforts were focused on American types.

Soon thereafter, collectors began scouring India for Spitfires and Israel for the P-51 Mustangs and Spitfires that had equipped this nation's air arm in the post-war years.

A decade and a half later, Latin and South America opened up and many former World War II aircraft were recovered from the region. Then, in the 1990s, after the Iron Curtain fell, a vast number of rare German and Russian aircraft were recovered from forests, lakes, and rivers, many of which have been restored to flying condition. All of these successes were accomplished by people wreckchasing.

In the first decade of the new millennium, the importance of preserving and recording historic aviation crash sites and the POW/MIA accounting movement came together. A number of universities recognized the need for formal archaeological training on how to examine and interpret aircraft crash sites. At the same time, various self- or privately-funded individuals and groups were searching for aircraft crash sites to document them, turn their locations over to the proper authorities for recovery of missing airmen and women, and to bring closure to families whose loved ones had been listed as missing in action.

On a different strata from the scholarly trained, professional aviation archaeologists are enthusiasts interested in aviation history and documenting the final resting places of aircraft, air crews, and in some cases passengers. Call them Wreckchasers or wreck hunters, the words are synonymous with enthusiasts who share a passion for the history, the human saga, and the environment where aircraft wrecks are found.

For those new to Wreckchasing, do not expect to find GPS coordinates or step-by-step directions to take a person to a crash site within the covers of this book. In *Wreckchasing 101*, the techniques and resources to enable enthusiasts to perform one's own research and find historic aircraft crash sites were shared along with a number of stories of aircraft lost and found. *Wreckchasing 102* builds upon that archive of information and presents the stories of sixteen historic aircraft crash sites ranging from a Boeing 247 airliner from the 1930s to a modern B-1A strategic bomber of the 1970s, along with a variety of civil and military aircraft types from the years in between.

Finding historic aircraft wrecks is ninety-five percent research and five percent field work. Make use of the resources available, network with other Wreckchasers, respect the sites, and do so safely. It will be a very rewarding experience.

United Air Lines Trip 3B was to take passengers from Spokane, Washington, to Seattle on June 7, 1934. Equipment for the flight was Boeing 247 NC13302, msn 1683, the first of the all-metal, low-wing transports delivered to the carrier, and accepted on March 30, 1933. (Boeing Historical Archives, HS-5009)

Chapter 1

Washington State's Killer Mountain Claims Three Airliners

Ed Davies

It was late Thursday afternoon, June 7, 1934. In the skies over the Pacific Northwest, a Boeing 247 airliner turned east, descending from the bright sunshine into the murky gray overcast that blanketed Seattle and extended inland to the foothills of the Cascade Mountains. Stewardess Marian Bennett clambered over the awkward wing spars that protruded through the narrow aisle, checking that each of the six passengers had adjusted their seat belts in preparation for landing. She was a trained nurse, hired by United Air Lines soon after the start of its in-flight service program. This afternoon, the passengers were quiet, white knuckled, acutely aware of the surging engine noise as the plane was buffeted by the turbulent air. The cabin darkened as the airliner plunged deeper and deeper into the moisture-laden clouds. Both Pilot Ben Redfield and Copilot Dwight Hansen leaned forward, peering through the rain-streaked windshield for the first glimpse of the ground below. When they broke out of the clouds, the horrified crew saw huge trees dead ahead, the forest ascending well above their line of vision.

Redfield firewalled the throttles and hauled back on the yoke, but just as the plane began to respond, it clipped the trees. The noise of the straining engines was joined by the tortured screeching of torn metal as the wings were sheared off during the headlong plunge through the forest of tall Canadian Hemlocks. Frightened passengers hung on for dear life, enduring the wild ride in the battered, but still intact, fuselage. What seemed an eternity later, the shattered remains of the once proud airliner came to a shuddering stop. There was no fire, though gasoline dripping from broken fuel lines would remain a potential hazard. The cacophony of noise and violent motion was over – the tragic scene now engulfed by the silence of the damp, remote forest.

Killer Mountain had claimed its first victim.

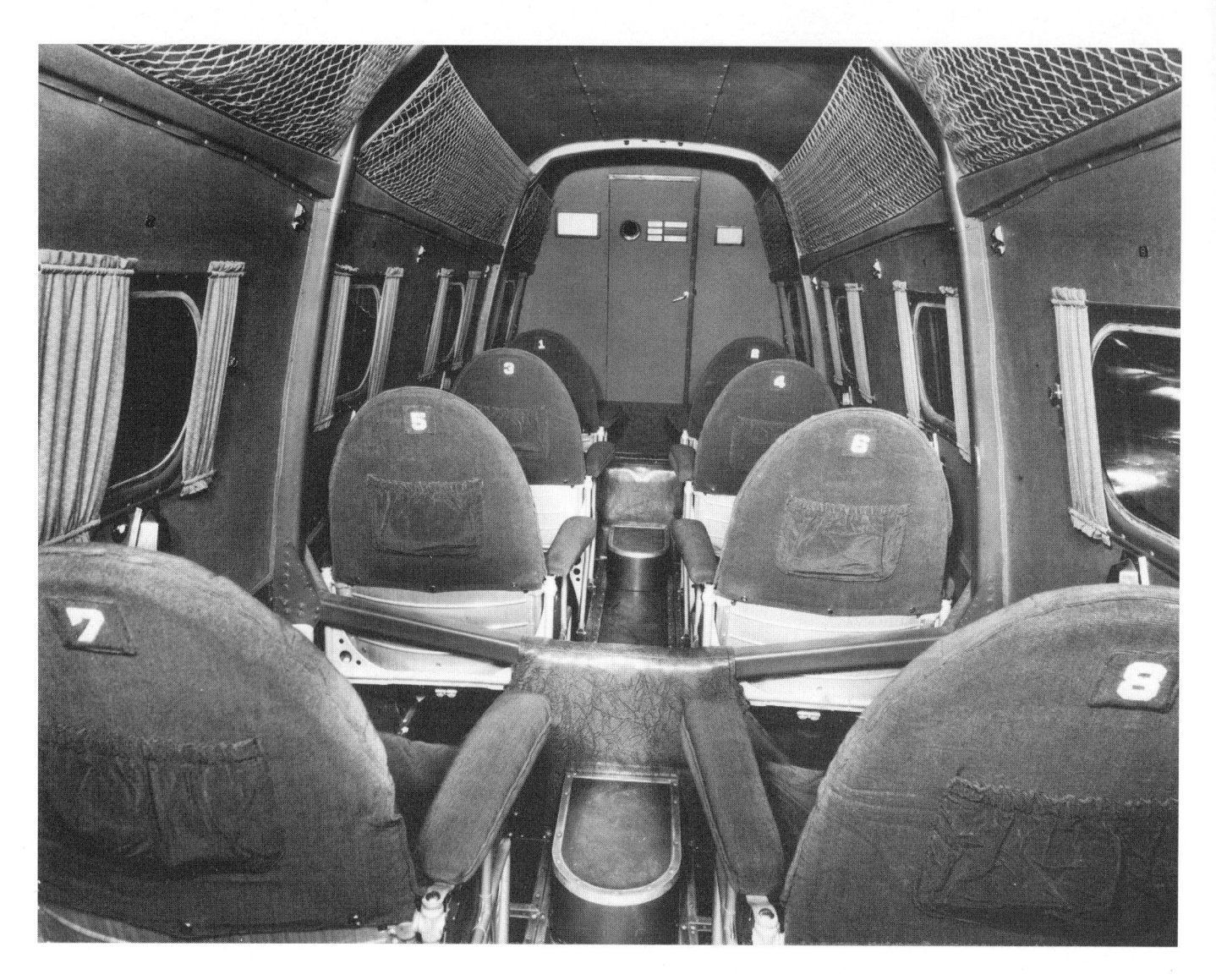

Interior of the Boeing 247 had the wing spar carring through the main cabin. Notice the spar is covered with leather, and has a step on both sides to enable passengers and flight attendants to walk through the cabin. (Boeing Historical Archives, 6252)

United Air Lines Trip 3B had originated in Spokane, in eastern Washington, then landed at Wenatchee, an intermediate flag stop to pick up four passengers. The departure was at 4:35 p.m., with an estimated flight time of forty-five minutes to Seattle. Weather was favorable until the plane reached the vicinity of the Snoqualmie Pass, where a low overcast persisted up to 3,500 feet. At this point, the pilot contacted Bob Ellis in the tower at Boeing Field and requested, and subsequently was given permission, to proceed "over the top" to the destination.

The plane was one of United's relatively new "Three-Mile-a-Minute" Boeing 247 ten-passenger airliners. This particular aircraft, NC13302, manufacturers serial number (msn) 1683, was the first of the 247s to be delivered to the airlines, going to the United conglomerate's Boeing Air Transport (BAT) division on March 30, 1933. These twin-engine monoplanes began flying United's transcontinental route in June 1933, quickly becoming the airliner of choice for speedy, comfortable, and safe transportation.

The following February, in 1934, the aviation industry, which depended on the government's generous air mail subsidy for a major part of its revenue, was thrown into turmoil. Claiming collusion between the major airlines, Postmaster General James J. Farley canceled all the existing air mail contracts. There followed a brief, disastrous attempt to use the United States Army to haul the mail. In March 1934, bids for a one-year period were once again requested. To meet the requirements for the new agreements, the various airlines in the Boeing/United company were re-organized under a single new operating company known as United Air Lines Inc. On May 1, 1934, the assets of BAT, Pacific Air Transport (PAT), and National Air Transport (NAT), including NC13302 were transferred to United Air Lines.

The Boeing 247 was a giant leap forward in transport technology. Overnight, the wire and strut-braced, fabric-covered biplanes that had been the mainstay of the airlines were rendered obsolete. An all-metal monoplane, the new design had internally braced wings with a close-cowled, 550-horsepower Pratt & Whitney Wasp engine faired into the leading edge on each side. Retractable landing gear, a heated, insulated cabin, and two-position, variable-pitch, three-blade propellers, were among the many innovations that were included in what became known as the first "Modern Airliner." Top speed was a phenomenal 182 mph. Despite being first in the field, the 247 had three shortcomings that limited production to seventy-five aircraft, and caused it to be displaced from the major routes within three years: The ten-passenger capacity was too small for transcontinental routes; the available horsepower in the Wasp engine was insufficient for a future stretch; and the entire initial production was committed to the airlines of the United group. Losing market share, the other major carriers desperately looked elsewhere for a competitive design, persuading the Douglas Aircraft Co. to build the larger, faster DC-2, and the twenty-one-passenger wide-body jumbo DC-3.

During its approach to Boeing Field, NC13302 crashed 30 miles east of the field in the Snoqualamie National Forest. Although the crash looks fatal, bruises and broken bones were the worst of the injuries. (Boeing Historical Archives, HS-4787)

NC13302 had crashed on the west slope of an as yet unnamed peak. The location was 30 miles east of Seattle's Boeing Field airport, in the Snoqualmie National Forest between Cedar Lake and the small logging town of Selleck. Miraculously all on board survived. The pilot was the most seriously injured with cuts, bruises, and a compound fracture of the left arm. Passenger Helen Curran's leg was broken and passenger Robert Clarke suffered a wrenched back. Despite leg and head injuries, Copilot Hansen took the compass out of the instrument panel and set off for help. Clambering down the steep slope, he reached the Pacific States Lumber Co. private railroad and contacted the company offices in Selleck from a trackside telephone. Loggers located him, escorted him the three miles to Selleck, from where he was transported by ambulance to a Seattle hospital. Meanwhile, a search-and-rescue party was organized to recover the rest of the crash victims, but darkness and the dense underbrush forced the team back to the railroad to await the coming dawn.

For Mercedes Boyd, a teacher at Winthrop in Okanogan County, her first plane ride turned out to be one traumatic experience after another. She started out with Hansen to seek help, but found herself unable to keep up with him while wearing her high-heel shoes. She had marked their trail with strips torn from her dress, but now on her own and with darkness falling, she made the wise decision to wait out the night under a tree rather than becoming hopelessly lost in the forest. Cold, wet, and hungry, she successfully found her way back to the plane at first light.

The injured were made as comfortable as possible. Emergency rations were retrieved from the plane, but a fire was out of the question because of the spilling gasoline. Huddled together, the remaining passengers and crew endured the long, cold night. Not knowing if Hansen had made it, with Mercedes Boyd missing, and no sign of a rescue party, it was now the turn of Seattle businessman P.C. Beezley to seek help. Leaving the plane at 4:30 a.m., he walked three miles through the rough terrain before he was picked up by the search team and whisked off to hospital for observation. Aided by directions from both Hansen and Beezley, lumber company superintendent Walter Gustke was the first of the search party to arrive about 10 a.m., at the crash site. Signal shots from his pistol quickly brought the others to render assistance to the cold, rain-soaked survivors.

Carefully the remaining passengers and crew were brought down the mountain. The injured and the others, who were all suffering from exposure, were taken to the Virginia Mason Hospital in Seattle. All eventually recovered from their traumatic experience.

An Accident Investigation Committee from United Air Lines and a representative from the Department of Commerce visited the crash site on June 10. Their preliminary findings reported that the pilot had failed to check his position before starting the descent and making a 180-degree turn to land towards the east. Their report harshly stated that: "The accident was due entirely to an error in judgment and thoughtlessness on the part of the pilot."

Though the fuselage was largely intact, a tribute to the strength of the new all-metal airliners, total salvage of the $65,000 airliner was considered impractical. It was however decided to retrieve selected items. Under the direction of United's Bob Ellis, a work party including mechanic Henry Strezlecki and a small group of local loggers, returned to the crash site. Over a period of two weeks, they hauled out portions of the two engines, control surfaces, the instrument panel, landing gear, and the wing to fuselage attachment pins. All had to be packed out, down the steep, heavily wooded terrain to the lumber company railroad, then to the Selleck terminal aboard small speeder cars.

The rest of the wreckage was left to be swallowed up by the lush growth of the forest floor. The story of the crash made newspaper headlines for two days and then was quickly forgotten. For two people, the incident created a lasting bond. Bob Ellis had worked the flight from the Boeing Field tower, had been one of the first to reach the incident site the morning after the crash, and led the parts recovery team. At the crash site, he had met Marian Bennett. On Christmas Eve 1934, the couple, who had been brought together by an airline disaster, were married.

Following World War II, safety over the nation-wide airways system was improved to accommodate the vastly increased number of larger, faster aircraft being operated by the major airlines and their non-scheduled competitors. In the Pacific Northwest, much of the increased traffic flew along the ninety-mile airborne freeway known as "Green Airway 2," between Ellensburg, Yakima, and Boeing Field in Seattle, directly over the inhospitable peaks of the Cascade Range. Though dwarfed by Mount Baker to the north and Mount Rainier to the south, Killer Mountain was poised like a coiled cobra, ready to strike at any aircraft that deviated from its assigned heading or altitude.

Civil Aeronautics Administration "radio range stations," at Ellensburg and near Boeing Field, transmitted a stream of Morse Code dot-dash As on one side of the airway center line and dash-dot Ns on the other. They merged into a continuous tone when the aircraft was "on the beam," along the centerline of the airway. The plane's position along the highway in the sky was established by "fan marker" transmitters located along the airway. They radiated a signal in the shape of a fan, extending vertically upward from the transmitting antenna with its major axis at right angles to the airway. The signal actuated a light on the instrument panel when the aircraft passed over the transmitter. Simultaneously, a modulated audio frequency Morse Code identifier was heard in the pilot's headset. The Hobart fan marker was fifteen miles east of the Seattle station and the Ellensburg fan marker thirty-eight miles west of Ellensburg. To safely clear Killer Mountain, the prescribed minimum altitude between these two fan markers was 8,000 feet. Only after passing these radio mileposts, were the transports cleared to begin their descent to the destination airport.

Miami Airlines DC-3 Goes Down

In the pre-dawn hours of Tuesday, April 14, 1953, Killer Mountain struck again. The aircraft was a Douglas DC-3. Wounded by engine problems, it strayed down to within the deadly grasp of the waiting peaks.

The Miami Airlines charter flight originated at National Airport in Washington, D.C., where the two pilots, Stewardess Adra Long, and twelve Army personnel boarded the aircraft. Two relief pilots, and ten additional soldiers, joined the flight at Wilkes-Barre, Pennsylvania. Their destination was Seattle, the northwest port of embarkation for troops bound for the Korean combat zone.

The aircraft, a twin-engine DC-3, was originally delivered to the United States Army Air Forces in May 1944, as C-47A transport. Declared surplus to requirements two years later, it was sold to Miami Airlines, converted for passenger operation, and registered NC65743 (msn 20432). The airline, which was founded in 1946 and was headquartered in Miami, held an operating certificate to engage in non-scheduled interstate, overseas, and foreign air transportation. They flew a number of DC-3 type aircraft.

The flight stopped at Cleveland for fuel and oil, and arrived at Chicago at 7:35 a.m. local time. Soon after takeoff from the Windy City, the crew decided to return

Operating as a charter flight on behalf of the U.S. Army, Miami Airlines' C-47A NC65473 was en route to Seattle from Washington, D.C. Engine troubles forced the plane down on Washington State's 'Killer Mountain.' (Larry Smalley via Davies DC-3 Collection)

because of problems with the left engine. The magneto on the offending powerplant was replaced and the journey resumed at 12:15 p.m. (CST). Further stops were made at Minneapolis and Fargo, North Dakota, where the relief pilots took over for the remainder of the journey. The full passenger load necessitated two more re-fueling stops, the first at Billings, Montana, and second Felt Field in Spokane. Departure on the final leg was just after midnight on Apr. 14. The flight plan called for Spokane to Ellensburg via Green Airway 2, and from there direct to Boeing Field, at an assigned altitude of 8,000 feet – well-clear of the lurking Cascade foothills.

Just after 2 a.m., April 14, the pilot of NC65743 called Seattle Center reporting that one of the plane's engines had failed and requested immediate clearance into Boeing Field. Transmissions from the aircraft were weak and difficult to understand, but it was apparent that the plane was now in icing conditions and losing altitude. The last communication was at 2:22 a.m. (PST), reporting that the flight was at 4,800 feet and dropping fast. Minutes later the airliner plunged into the tall trees.

The aircraft was descending with wings level, on a northwesterly heading when first the right-wing tip struck a tree and was torn off. The plane decelerated rapidly as tree after tree progressively tore away both wings. Striking the hillside, the cockpit was crushed, immediately killing both pilots. The fuselage disintegrated into three parts, tearing all twenty-eight seats from their attachments, throwing occupants about in the dark twisted cabin. After what must have seemed an eternity, the headlong plunge crunched to a shattering stop. Silence fell over the snow-covered mountain, broken only by the cries of the injured passengers. Approximately seven miles east of Selleck, the survivors were at 3,500 feet, less than 500 feet from the summit of Killer Mountain and the comparative safety of the flatlands beyond.

Search and rescue teams, many trained for just such an emergency, were alerted when it became apparent that the crippled transport had crashed. However, hampered by darkness and the remote mountainous location, the wreck site remained undetected until the following morning. A Civil Air Patrol Cessna 170 from Renton Municipal Airport, one of many aircraft that resumed the search at first light, spotted the dark scar in the snow just before noon. The position was flashed to the frustrated ground crews and waiting Coast Guard helicopters. An hour later, Sandra Long and Army Private Odell Mathews, both of whom had left the crash site to seek help, were sighted walking down the mountain. They were picked up and transported by a Coast Guard helicopter to Selleck where the two-story wood-frame school building was being converted into a makeshift hospital. The children had been sent home with requests for cots and bedding, and as the news spread, their mothers pitched in to set-up the care center and prepared food and coffee. These first two survivors confirmed that others were alive, although many were badly injured.

Time was now of the essence, for although it had stopped snowing, the injured and dying had already spent twelve hours on the frigid mountain. Doctors, nurses, medical supplies and equipment all poured in from Seattle, the 13th Coast Guard District, and McChord Air Force Base. Lumberjacks from the nearby logging camps hurried to bulldoze a trail to a point 1,000 yards below the crash site. Spurred on by the screams of the injured, rescuers urgently ploughed through deep snow on the steep, brush-covered slopes. First on the site was Robert Chauvin of the United States Coast Guard, who had been dropped by helicopter within two miles of the accident site and had struggled the rest of the way on foot. He administered morphine to the most seriously injured and, together with two paramedics from McChord who arrived soon afterwards, began the immediate task of stabilizing the victims. Medical supplies, blankets, and sleeping bags were parachuted in and the delicate operation to get the soldiers off the mountain to the triage center in the Selleck school swung into high gear.

The next soldier to reach Selleck was Private Robert Lynch, whose feet had been almost severed. Fashioning a sled stretcher from the aircraft door, State Fire Warden Don Puckett, Logger Tom Mattioda, and other local volunteers carefully man-handled Lynch down the almost vertical 1,000 yards to the cleared trail. A helicopter then air lifted him to Selleck and onto Madigan Army Hospital at Fort Lewis in Tacoma. The helicopters were grounded as darkness began to fall, and trucks and ambulances bucked over the rough trails to bring out the last nine men. Twelve frantic hours would elapse before Private Joseph Smariga, the 19th and last of the crash victims, was carried into the temporary Selleck hospital at 11:30 p.m.

The two pilots, Captain A.J. Lerette and William Harshman, along with four soldiers, died at the crash site. A fifth passenger died later of injuries suffered in the crash. Examination of the wreckage indicated that the left engine failed first, due to the failure of both master rod bearings. This engine was shut down and the propeller feathered. The resulting higher load then initiated a similar failure of the right engine. A last ditch attempt was made to restart the number one engine, and it was partially unfeathered and generating some power when the aircraft struck the hillside. The Civil Aeronautics Board investigation determined that the probable cause of the crash was the progressive failure of both engines, due to the lack of compliance with the proper maintenance standards.

Incredibly, the aircraft records show that Miami Airlines reputedly recovered and rebuilt this DC-3. The aircraft was re-registered as N3935C. It later saw service in Canada and South America. The airliner was last reported in 1972, derelict at Bogota. Despite this paper trail, there remains a big question mark on the whether a meaningful quantity of the aircraft wreckage was ever salvaged.

Dormant for almost twenty years, Killer Mountain had struck again. Only ten days later it would viciously claim yet another victim.

Shortly after World War II, the U.S. government leased a number of its surplus transports to GIs who wanted to start airlines. Known as non-scheduled carriers, dozens sprung up in the late 1940s and early 1950s. Seen at Oakland, Calif., in February 1953, just two months before her final flight, C-46F N1693M was operated by American Air Transport of Miami, Florida. (William T. Larkins)

The Loss of American Air Transport's C-46 N1693M

American Air Transport Inc. of Miami, Florida., leased three C-46F Curtiss Commandos from the United States Air Force. Registered N1693M, msn 22498, the airliner that eventually crashed was one of three leased aircraft. Though of World War II vintage, the C-46 was still popular among non-scheduled carriers for both freight and passenger services. Powered by a pair of 2,000-horsepower Pratt & Whitney R-2800-75, 14-cylinder, air-cooled radial engines, the C-46 could carry up to forty passengers.

Two ships loaded with troops returning from the Far East war zone had recently docked at Seattle. American Air Transport was one of several carriers chartered to fly the soldiers on the final leg of the long journey to their home bases. The C-46 was being staged from Columbia, North Carolina, to Boeing Field to begin the airlift. The only people aboard for the ferry flight were the two pilots and a second crew consisting of Captain Maurice Booska, the chief pilot of the company, and First Officer Donald Dwelley. This relief crew had taken over the controls at Cheyenne, Wyoming.

The flight proceeded uneventfully to Cheyenne, where it was serviced, took on a full load of 1,200 gallons of 100-octane fuel, and departed at 8:43 p.m. (MST). Over Boise, the Seattle weather was requested and an Instrument Flight Rules (IFR) flight plan was filed to the destination at an altitude of 12,000 feet. Near Yakima the flight was cleared to descend to 10,000 feet, and then was cleared to descend and maintain 8,000 feet. The flight passed over Ellensberg at 12:34 a.m. (PST) at an altitude of 8,000 feet, and flying IFR.

The pilot contacted Seattle Center at 12:47 a.m., April 23, 1953, and was given the following clearance: "Nectar one six nine three metro, you are cleared to cross Hobart at 8,000. Seattle at or above 4,000, maintain 4,000. No delay expected, contact Seattle approach control, over Hobart for further clearance, over." The recording of the

Cedar River Watershed

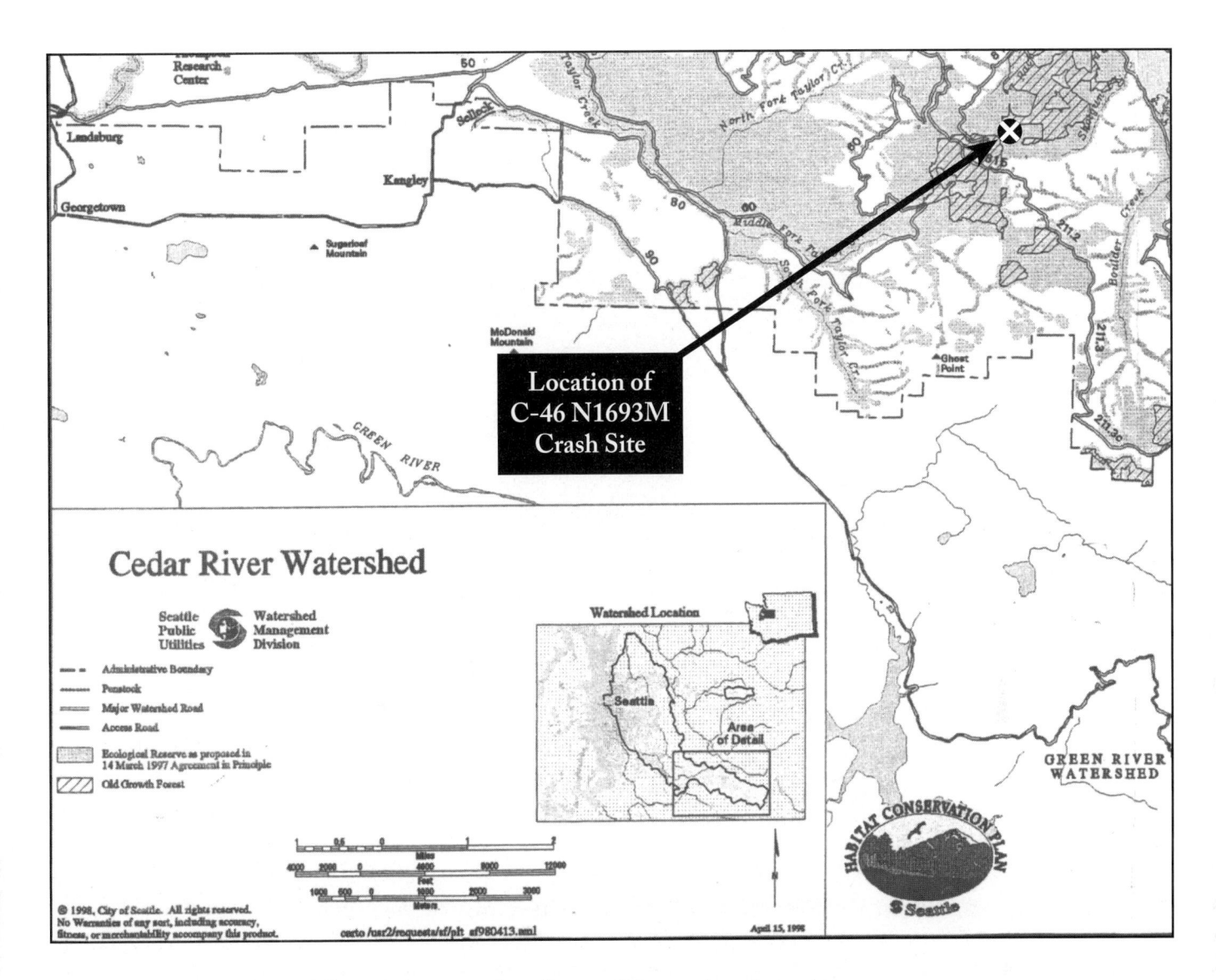

Location of C-46 N1693M Crash Site

read back raised the first red flag on the impending disaster. "Roger, cleared to – (three second pause) – cross there 4,000 or above the range station, Ah, 4,000, report Hobart to you." The controller immediately responded: "Negative. Report Hobart to Seattle approach control." The part of the pilot's confusing readback that intimated an altitude of 4,000 feet over the Hobart fan marker went unchallenged. There was no further contact from the aircraft. Search and rescue activities were instituted when the flight was overdue at its Boeing Field destination, having failed to report over Hobart.

At first light Thursday planes from throughout the area took off to look for the downed transport. However, heavy cloud cover was blanketing the Cascades, forcing the aircraft to return to base, leaving only the ground crews to continue the futile search in the desolate snow-covered mountains. Friday morning the weather improved and Civil Air Patrol member Kiyo Yabuki and his observer Paul Perry, on their first-ever flying rescue mission, spotted a wisp of smoke in the distance. Turning to investigate, they sighted a survivor waving frantically to attract the plane's attention. Making sure that the downed airman knew that they had seen him, Yabuki headed for the nearest cow pasture, landed, and dashed over to a farm house to telephone his report of the sighting. With the rough field too short for a departure with both onboard, Perry hitchhiked out to North Bend Airport where he was picked up by Yabuki. The pair then headed for the crash site.

The C-46 crash site can be seen in the small clearing within the new growth forest. Notice inclination of the terrain. (Ed Davies)

The C-46 had first struck a large tree, approximately 210 feet east of the crest of the Killer Mountain. Its momentum carried the fuselage over the top of the mountain, shedding metal parts as it cut a 900-foot swath through the forest. The recent wreckage of the Miami Airlines DC-3 lay only a mile away. The plane had been on course at 4,000 feet, below the minimum prescribed altitude for aircraft flying between the two airway markers. Examination of both of the engines revealed that they were developing appreciable power and the propellers were in the cruising range when the Commando crashed.

The cockpit section of the aircraft was smashed as it careened over the mountain top, instantly killing Captain Booska and First Officer Dwelley. Captain Schroeder and Copilot James Gilbert, who were riding in the back of the plane, were thrown clear and received only minor injuries. Loggers who reached the crash site just after 1:30 p.m. on Saturday afternoon, were astonished to find two survivors near the badly damaged remains of the aircraft. Treated at the site by paramedics who parachuted in, the two pilots were strapped onto litters and carefully carried down the snow-covered mountainside. In a small clearing at the 2,500-foot level, a Coast Guard helicopter was waiting to transport them to Boeing Field. Once on the ground, they were taken by ambulance to the Virginia Mason Hospital for observation.

The Civil Aeronautics Board determined that the probable cause was: "The pilot's misunderstanding of the clearance, failure to check en route altitude against available charts, and descent below prescribed minimum en route altitude."

Killer Mountain had claimed its last victims.

Artifacts found at the crash site of C-46 N1693M include a hydraulic pressure guage, a seat back, and a part number data plate. (Ed Davies)

Seattle-Tacoma Airport was officially opened in July 1949 and is Seattle's main commercial airport. Boeing Field is now predominantly used by corporate and general aviation aircraft. The Boeing Aircraft Co. uses the field for test, acceptance, and delivery flights of 737 and 757 airliners built at nearby Renton. Newer, pressurized passenger planes operate at altitudes far above that of the Cascade Mountain range peaks eliminating this peak as a hazard to navigation. The town of Selleck is virtually deserted, the logging mill and school long closed down. Today, all three aircraft crash sites are inaccessibly sequestered in the prohibited wilderness area of the Seattle Water District.

The crumpled fuselage of American Air Transport's N1693M as seen nearly 50 years after the plane crashed in the wilderness east of Seattle. (Ed Davies)

N1693M's tail folded over to starboard during the crash. The registration number is barely visible in this photo. (Ed Davies)

The Revelations of Wreckchasing

The author's investigation of the "Killer Mountain" wrecks began when a database search of accident sites in the region surrounding Seattle's Boeing Field exposed a small cluster just south of the Chester Morse Lake. The database, built up over the past fifteen years, lists the incidents by date, location that includes the state and nearest city, and aircraft type. This information is backed up by hard copies of the official accident investigation reports, sometimes accompanied by contemporary newspaper or magazine articles, all chronological. In the case of the United 247, the accident report was a document of the findings of the airline's own Accident Investigation Committee, which was made up of seven managers and pilots from United's Western Division. The reports on the other two incidents were issued by the Civil Aeronautics Board.

Armed with an accurate date, the next stop was the library to search the newspaper microfilm for relevant reports, and to make hard copies. In this case, the newspapers were the *Seattle Times* and *Post-Intelligencer*. Later, during a visit to Wenatchee, the obliging staff at the public library helped find the microfilm for the June 1934 *Wenatchee Daily World*. Here were the personal stories of several passengers from the local area who had been aboard the fateful United flight.

The probable locations of the wreck sites, all from pre-GPS days, were far from precise. The topography had changed by increased water storage, and the name of the dominant lake – just north of the sites – had been changed from Cedar to Chester Morse. All three sites were near the geographic center of the city of Seattle, which owns the Cedar River Watershed. This approximately 90,000-acre wilderness provides almost two-thirds of the drinking water for metropolitan Seattle, and a very small portion of its electricity from the hydro-electric plant below the dam at the western end of the lake. To maintain water quality, the area is off limits to the general public. The slopes were logged over many years, and the area crisscrossed with primitive dirt logging roads and railroad tracks. Timber cutting was considerably reduced during the 1990s and the most recent Habitat Conservation Plan forbids any future logging in the watershed. Many of the already deteriorating dirt roads are now permanently closed, and steps have been taken to stop road dirt from washing into protected salmon habitat.

Remote, inaccessible areas are the preferred domain of the wreckchaser. With this territory comes the probability that at least some remnants of even the oldest crash remain at the site. First there was more research, and then a little luck is needed to follow a cold, fifty-year-old trail.

The Boeing Co. archives held photographs of the 247 crash site taken soon after the incident in June 1934. The friendly folks at the Museum of Flight archives and library added their knowledge, sifted from its huge collection of aviation history. The luck came when someone mentioned that Bob Ellis was still alive. The author, accompanied by Tom Lubbesmeyer from The Boeing Co. archives, visited with Ellis and heard his first-hand account of the 1934 crash.

The ultimate objective of this wreckchase was to find the aircraft's remains, and time was running out. We were fortunate enough to have the Watershed Management Division of the City of Seattle allow us one-time access to the area accompanied by Watershed Inspector Lloyd Buster as our guide and wilderness mentor. The day was similar to that when the 247 crashed. The road to the mountain was shrouded in a thick overcast out of which squeezed a constant miserable drizzle. Buster assured us that we would climb above all this. As his trusty four-wheel-drive vehicle took us over grass-lined, barely passable dirt roads, we broke out into the sunshine. We were luckier than pilot Redfield. As the morning wore on, the overcast pulled back to the coast, leaving just lingering fingers of white mist in the canyons that led down to Puget Sound. The lack of a precise location loomed large as the afternoon wore on.

With Tom Lubbesmeyer and Cory Graff, then from the Museum of Flight, we clambered over fallen gray tree trunks and through dense brush. There was a brief flurry of excitement as we came across a six-foot section of aluminum, but closer inspection revealed that it was from the wing of a much smaller aircraft. We didn't have to worry about poisonous snakes as there are none west of the Cascades. If there had been any, they would have been eaten alive by the mosquitoes that were doing a pretty good job on us. Eventually we spotted the twisted remains of a white fuselage on the west side of a steep clear-cut slope. Way down was the tail, severed from the rest of the plane, and marked many years ago with a red cross by the Civil Air Patrol. Further up the slope was a twenty-foot section of the fuselage with several of the canvas covered seats still inside. We scrambled down through the shoulder-high, thorn-covered brush. We tried to push our way around the battered metal shapes to take photographs. The registration N1693M, was still visible on the tail. It was the American Air Transport C-46.

Flushed with success, we began the difficult climb out. Two steps forward, slip one back. Breathless, we reached the top with just enough strength to flee from the mosquitoes to the safety of the cab of the Ford Expedition. Two wrecks to go, but we'd had enough exploring this day. Over beer and pizza, we talked over the strategy of the next visit. With lots of mosquito repellent, some day we will return to Killer Mountain.

An unidentified B-17C as 40-2047 would have appeared before it crashed. Many of the stateside Army Air Corps B-17Cs were repainted with warpaint through the late spring and summer of 1941, most when modified by Boeing to the B-17D configuration. This B-17C lacks engine cowl flaps, indicating it was probably repainted at an AAC depot before it was sent back to Boeing for modifications. The 19th Bomb Group B-17Cs and Ds sent to the Philippines in the fall of 1941, ironically, retained their natural metal finishes when deployed and many remained unpainted as the war began. The markings on the tail of this B-17C indicates it was assigned to the 2nd Bomb Group, possibly making it s/n 40-2074. (Boeing Historical Archives)

Chapter 2

In-Flight Break-up Claims B-17C Flying Fortress

Scott A. Thompson

It was just another day, a Sunday morning in early November 1941. Though the United States was still a nation at peace, the news was full of impending war clouds billowing on the horizon. The Sunday morning newspaper told that the Japanese were rushing a special envoy to Washington, D.C., to deal with the "serious situation prevailing." The German government, meanwhile, was refusing to pay an American claim of $3 million for a ship, the *Robin Moor*, that the German Navy had sunk earlier in the summer. Pearl Harbor was but five weeks in the future.

This Sunday morning Air Corps First Lieutenant Leo M. Walker, fighting ominous weather, was trying to fly his four-engine B-17C and crew safely from Reno, Nevada, to McClellan Field near Sacramento, California. Though only a short distance by air miles, his route crossed the stark backbone of California: the rugged Sierra Nevada. The Sierras stretch 300 miles along the eastern edge of California, with jagged, snow-covered granite peaks jutting defiantly over 14,000 feet above the sea level valleys to the west. The range's anchor point is the jewel-like Lake Tahoe nestled in an alpine valley 6,000 feet above sea level. In the 1840s, the Sierras blocked emigrants trying to reach California from the east; for eons the mountains prevented eastward-moving storm systems from reaching Nevada. The airborne battles fought between the Sierra Nevadas and moist weather systems coming off the Pacific produce routinely vicious and often deadly storms, one of which now lay before Walker and his crew. Before this Sunday was over, Walker's B-17 would be reduced to shards of aluminum spread across the high Sierras as yet another victim claimed by the aviator's unforgiving foe.

The task that had been set before Lt. Walker two days earlier by his commander at the Seventh Bombardment Group Headquarters at Fort Douglas, Utah, was simple

'C' model B-17 Flying Fortress in flight showing the 'bath tub' enclosure, which preceeded the ball turret installation of later models. (Author's Collection)

enough. He was ordered to ferry a B-17C, Army s/n 40-2047, from his station at the Salt Lake Airport to Sacramento for a change-out of the number three engine at McClellan's Sacramento Air Depot, a flight of about 600 miles. The nine-man crew included several mechanics that were to assist in the engine change. Walker, who joined the Air Corps from Hattiesburg, Mississippi, had earned his wings nearly a year and a half earlier. He and his copilot, Second Lt. John Mode, planned out a route across the dry lakes of western Utah and scrub desert of eastern Nevada, over Reno and the Sierras, and down into the Sacramento Valley. Departing Halloween morning, October 31, the crew enjoyed a routine flight until passing Reno. West of Reno, though, the crew was slammed by an early winter storm boiling up the west face of the Sierras and instead of a routine arrival at McClellan, they were forced to divert back into Reno. There, they sat out the weather for two days, looking for improvement.

The B-17C they were flying was one of only thirty-eight built and had been delivered from the Boeing factory at Boeing Field in Seattle fifteen months earlier on Aug. 23, 1940. It was the sixth B-17C delivered by Boeing. The B-17Cs sported the distinctive small shark-finned tail of the early B-17 series, quite different from the broad and distinctive dorsal fin of the B-17E and later versions of the famed Boeing Flying Fortress. The B-17Cs and B-17Ds built in 1940 could well be considered the adolescent versions of the B-17 bomber; going away was the naiveté of the mid-1930s design, with its few 0.30-cal. guns and vulnerable gas tanks, yet lacking the heavily-gunned power turrets, armor plating, and function-over-form utility of the fully matured B-17G.

After the United States Army Air Corps accepted 40-2047 in the late summer of 1940, it was sent straight to the Sacramento Air Depot and remained there for nearly six months, apparently in storage as it was not flown. However, twenty sibling B-17Cs were shunted off to join the Royal Air Force for combat over Europe. The B-17C, the Army Air Corps freely acknowledged, was not up to the task of performing modern aerial warfare at the level being practiced by the British and the Germans over Europe in 1941. The official Army Air Forces recommendation was that the RAF use their B-17Cs only for training and leave combat to the new B-17Es that would start rolling off the production line in September. Nonetheless, the desperate RAF threw their B-17Cs, dubbed Fortress Is, into the fray with predictably dismal results.

Line up of B-17C or Ds, probably in mid-to-late 1941. Because the B-17C was upgraded to the D configuration it is difficult to determine which of the series these aircraft are. Though the location is not confirmed, the hangar style in the background would suggest either March Field or Hamilton Field, both in California. (Author's collection)

Meanwhile, 40-2047 remained at McClellan through April 1941. In early May it was flown back to the Boeing factory in Seattle where it was refitted to the newer B-17D standard. Cowl flaps were installed on each of the four engine nacelles, and B.F. Goodrich self-sealing fuel cells replaced the original aluminum tanks in each wing. Numerous other small equipment upgrades were also added. At the completion of the modifications, 40-2047 was repainted by Boeing with the standardized camouflage colors adopted by the Army in early 1941, the colorful pre-war natural metal finish and markings giving way to ominous olive drab and grey. It was then returned to the Air Corps and assigned to the Salt Lake Airdrome at Fort Douglas, Utah, attached to the headquarters squadron of the 7th Bomb Group.

As 1941 began there were two western bomb groups equipped with B-17s, the 7th Bomb Group at Salt Lake City and the Nineteenth Bomb Group at Albuquerque, New Mexico, with detachments at March Field in California. With the first rumblings of war, the 7th Bomb Group began deploying squadrons to Hamilton Field (near San Francisco), California. In early October 1941, the 19th Bomb Group was moved, en masse, to Clark Field in the Philippines to beef up the United States' defenses in the

B-17C 40-2049 Skipper at Bellows Field, Territory of Hawaii, on December 7, 1941. Skipper was one of the B-17s flying from California to Hawaii that arrived during the Japanese attack that Sunday morning. Had B-17C 40-2047 not broken up over the Sierra Nevada Mountains, she, too, would have been in the B-17 flight arriving over Pearl Harbor during the attack. (Veronico Collection)

Bathtub ventral gun position as seen on a production B-17

turbulence, precipitation, and airframe icing. The flight engineer, Sgt. Eugene Clemens, worked with the pilots in trying to restore full power to the number one engine and the instrument vacuum system. The other six men in the airplane, spread out in the nose compartment and aft of the bomb bay, were alerted to put their parachutes on. Those in the nose were instructed to move to the tail for a possible bail-out.

All the while Walker continued to climb. As he passed through 18,000 feet, the copilot later remembered that Walker made some minor pitch changes with the control column, and that the airplane began to sink. Walker, trying to continue the climb, pulled back the control column a bit. The copilot recalled that the airspeed still read 150 mph (possibly due to an iced-over pitot-static system), but the four-engine bomber suddenly stalled and, with a violent wing drop, fell into a spin.

No one had to tell the crew it was time to get out but as they began to scramble for exits centrifugal force from the spinning airplane pinned them to the fuselage walls. For those in back, near the tail, an exit was provided when the fuselage broke in two just aft of the wing. Some were thrown out at that point, while others were able to jump. One of the passengers, Private Fred Pekuri, recalled the process in his understated comments about getting out of the aft fuselage: "I was thrown on the floor and held down there. I made a dive for the door and pulled the emergency release, but the door failed to open. I kicked it with my feet and beat on it with my hands, and immediately the ship keeled over and the tail section sheared off aft of the radio compartment. I noticed this occurrence and crawled over the sheared portion of the ship, waited about five seconds, and pulled the rip-cord and the chute opened."

The pilots and flight engineer in front were trying to get out the emergency hatch in the cockpit roof. Sergeant Clemens, the flight engineer, grabbed at the hatch handle but was thrown to the floor and pinned. Mode later recalled that after the plane fell into a spin, they "knew we would have to abandon the airplane and we unfastened our safety belts, and Sergeant Clemens and I both reached for the hatch. We managed to open the hatch, and the airplane went wild. I was thrown on the floor and was completely helpless, and my ankle was injured. I think Sergeant Clemens was thrown out at this time. I was held on the floor for a few seconds, and while I was there, I could hear the airplane breaking up. Then I was thrown clear of the plane, and I saw the wreckage of the airplane before my chute opened. I saw one large piece that looked

The wing came to rest inverted, with the bomb bay facing toward the sky. The above photo shows the front of the center section, which would face the nose of the bomber, while the lower photo looks toward the aft end of the bomb bay. (Scott Thompson)

27

like the fuselage with the tail and wings torn off, but I am not certain of this as the visibility was so bad." Walker, however, was unable to get out of the cockpit and went in with the airplane.

Eight of the nine crewmembers bailed out, something of a miracle given the violent nature of the bomber's destruction. Suspended from their life saving parachutes, each survivor recalled hearing the sounds of the bomber wrenching itself apart in its death dive, though visual contact was quickly lost in the clouds. One passenger, Private Harold Salisbury, recalled that after he "had bailed out, I could hear the ship tearing up. The engines sound like they were running away." At some point the left wing broke off just outboard of the number one engine, while three of the four nacelles and engines also separated during the break-up. Small parts of the bomber fluttered around the descending parachutes as a potentially deadly escort. The falling wreckage was spread out over a one by two-mile area in a remote area twenty miles west of Lake Tahoe.

Incredibly, all eight survivors landed in relative safety in the desolate, tree and granite-covered wilderness. Each man landed in isolation, some dropping freely through pine trees while others snagged in high limbs above the ground. Several received minor injuries to ankles and legs during the landing to add to the minor injuries suffered as they exited the airplane. Yelling for each other, a few were able to gather together. All were able to walk and began to search for help. Several stumbled to a remote cabin on a local ranch called the Upper Bassi where some startled cowboys then heard news of the crash. They were able to help the downed crew and alerted authorities of the accident. Three other crewmen, after searching for help for hours, finally located an unoccupied cabin where they took shelter. They were found by a search party at 3:30 a.m., some fifteen hours after the crash.

The more seriously injured crewmembers were transported the forty-five miles to the nearest town and, eventually, to the McClellan Field hospital. The uninjured in the crew joined a massive search party to try to find the only missing crewman: Lt. Leo Walker. It took two days of trekking through the remote area for the searchers to find the remains of the cockpit section and, sadly, Walker.

An accident committee was convened within a week at McClellan Field, and the report was completed on November 12, 1941. The committee concluded, not surprisingly, that Lt. Walker was mostly to blame for the accident, primarily for attempting to continue the flight to McClellan after encountering communication and navigation problems. Also, the committee noted the pilot's "lack of experience with the equipment under the conditions he was, then, operating."

Not noted in the report but perhaps enlightening of nature's fury: the Sunday that saw a B-17C fall victim to weather claimed several other military planes: the newspaper accounts of the day note three Hamilton Field P-40s crashing in the San Francisco Bay area as a result of the same storm, which also claimed several BT-13 trainers in the Central Valley.

Within a few days of the investigation's conclusion, the 7th Bomb Group was scrambling in preparation for a trans-Pacific ferry flight to the Philippines. A few weeks later the nation was embroiled in a World War. Coincidentally, unarmed elements of the 7th Bomb Group arrived in Hawaii in the midst of the Japanese attack on Pearl Harbor during the first leg of their ferry flight. In the end, the personal scars of the accident and the loss of Lt. Walker were quickly obscured by the rising crescendo of war, much as the lonely mountainside absorbed the broken pieces of a bomber as its own.

B-17C Crash Site Today

The research into the crash which took the young life of Lt. Leo Walker and broke apart his bomber was sparked by the individual aircraft history contained in Roger Freeman's *The Flying Fortress Story*. The region between Sacramento and Lake Tahoe has become a popular camping area, with numerous man-made dams and reservoirs being constructed to harness the essential lifeblood of California: water.

Taking a local historical interest, a review was made of period newspaper accounts. Upon receipt of the Army accident committee's report, a decision was taken to try to locate the crash site. A fairly detailed map of wreckage was included in the accident report; an attempt was then made to match this up to the current topographical chart published by the U.S. Coast and Geodetic Survey. Geographical details matched, including the location of the Upper Bassi Ranch and Tells Creek, along which much of the wreckage fell. The area remains almost as inaccessible now as it did nearly eighty years ago when the accident occurred. There are some rugged jeep trails which lie along the perimeter of the wreckage area, but these were found to be unusable. A foot trail extends into the area also, and this proved more promising. Examining the chart, it was determined that a hike of about two miles from a forest service road on the trail would bring a hiker to Tells Creek. A lateral move south along the creek for one-quarter mile and then continuing parallel to the original trail for one-half mile would provide access into the area where much of the wreckage had fallen.

The first effort was unsuccessful; the meager trail led through tall stands of pine trees but was nearly overgrown with lush vegetation. It was obvious that any deviation from the trail for more than a few hundred feet would risk disorientation and, given the remote location, a potentially disastrous result. The banks of Tells Creek were

View from the tail looking forward, with the starboard horizontal stabilizer on the right. The structure in the foreground is part of the mid-fuselage peeled away from the aft section. In this view several people have opened up a view of the interior of the aft fuselage by lifting up the flattened section. (Author)

View of the number three nacelle, the only remaining nacelle attached to the wing. All the engines, three nacelles, and the landing gear were ripped away during the breakup. (Author)

overgrown and inaccessible and any effort made to parallel the creek difficult. Two trekkers, this author and his eager eleven-year-old son, probed other areas around the trail where aircraft remains might be found but the searching proved fruitless. Clearly, the main wreckage area had to be reached if any remains of the aircraft were to be located.

Taking advantage of modern satellite navigation, a second attempt was warranted. Using a versatile GPS hand-held receiver, another attempt was made to locate the main wreckage area the following month. On a warm California summer morning this author set out again on the trail accompanied by his eighteen-year-old son. Leaving the trail at Tells Creek, a course was set through dense underbrush and rising terrain. A half mile later, while cresting a ridgeline, a metallic object could be seen part way down the far hill. Upon closer examination, it was obviously a fuel tank cell from the B-17C. It appeared undisturbed after nearly sixty years, with one end crushed by impact but with a clearly marked Goodrich fuel bladder visible within the aluminum tank. Other plates identified it as a Boeing-built part: a tangible part of the B-17C had been located. Searching out around the fuel tank, no further evidence of the aircraft could be found. We hiked further down the hill on our plotted course and began climbing another, steeper hill. Stepping around fallen trees in the dark shadows of the hillside, a tiny glint of metal revealed several other pieces nearly buried under pine needles and dirt. These turned out to be part of an engine nacelle, the top fairing at the aft end of the nacelle as it blends into the wing. It appeared the part was painted black that, later, was presumed to have been faded-to-black olive drab. We hiked further up the hill and onto the subsequent ridgeline and began searching again, as this was the area where the cockpit and nose section had probably fallen. Despite a widespread search, no further evidence of wreckage was found. It was decided to return to the area of the first two finds and put off any search for the four engines, all of which had fallen in the same area further down the hill. There was some indication in the newspaper accounts that the engines had been removed and salvaged by a McClellan work crew in 1941.

Returning to the area where the nacelle parts had been found, another distant glint of aluminum brought us to one of the main landing gear and tire. The oleo strut was as shiny as the day the airplane was built, while the tire was off its rim. It was a tread-less casing peculiar to the prewar B-17s. Etchings in the tire indicated we were not the first to find the wheel and tire. We decided then to walk back toward an area where the wings and center section had reportedly impacted, some distance away on the other side of Tells Creek. Setting the GPS course, we descended from the ridgeline through thick brush and tangled fallen trees to cross the narrow creek. As we approached the creek, we could see a large piece of wreckage clearly on the other side, about a hundred feet from the edge of the creek. We crossed the creek and approached the wreckage. As expected, it consisted of the entire right wing, the bomb-bay, and half the left wing. The wing was laying bottom side up, and it initially appeared that the airplane was unpainted and not the camouflage grey undersurface we anticipated. However, on closer examination it appears the grey paint had faded away on all exposed surfaces, revealing the Army markings and insignia originally applied at the factory. Areas protected from the elements showed clear evidence of grey paint applied. The wreckage parts were in amazingly good condition, given that they had been on the ground exposed to the elements for many decades. The aluminum shined brightly and interior parts still bore grease-penciled markings made by factory workers or mechanics in the field.

Three of the four nacelles were gone from the wing's leading edge, confirming what the accident committee reported. The bomb-bay doors could be easily pulled opened, revealing the crushed upper part of the fuselage center section. Others had visited this wreckage before: small graffiti names were scratched into the bulkhead where the cockpit had once attached. Some names had dates back to the early 1950s. Others had apparently come with a more utilitarian purpose as most removable hardware, such as wiring harnesses, hydraulic actuators, and other small parts, were salvaged. The right-wing flap and aileron were also present, though the wingtip was mangled. Bits of fabric still clung to the aileron's aluminum framework. Examination of the fabric showed grey paint over doped aluminum pigment. On the other end of the wreckage, the jagged edge of the left wing outboard of the number one engine revealed the violent nature with which the outboard section had parted company with the airframe.

Several weeks later another trip was made into the area by some local aviation archeologists. The aft fuselage section from the B-17 radio compartment to the tail cone was finally located along with the right horizontal stabilizer and the vertical fin. The fuselage section was found crushed flat halfway up a steep hill. The fuselage skin from the radio room back to almost the waist gun emplacements was peeled apart and lay largely buried around the aft section. Pulling the top of the fuselage upward revealed the interior of the aft fuselage, again in surprisingly good condition. Remains of the waist gun windows and bathtub gun position were also located. The Army Air Corps insignia, blue disc, white star, and red disc, was quite apparent on the side of the fuselage protected from the elements. The vertical fin had clearly identifiable pencil markings where a long-forgotten ground crewman had laid out numbers for never-painted squadron identification numbers.

The crash site is quite remote and the condition of the wreckage would likely preclude any useful parts being drawn from the airframe. An extensive search of the likely area where the cockpit and forward fuselage had fallen was conducted but no additional airframe parts were located.

P-39Q 44-3586 suffered a gear-up landing on December 29, 1944. The aircraft was repaired and ready for flight on Februray 5, 1945, when 2Lt. Paul Coleman climbed into the Airacobra to fly a gunnery camera mission from the Las Vegas Army Air Field. (USAAF)

Chapter 3

P-39 Airacobra Gamble: Lost on a Las Vegas Training Mission

James D. Scroggins III

On February 5, 1945, Second Lt. Paul Coleman was one of many pilots preparing for a gunnery camera mission at the Las Vegas Army Air Field (LVAAF), Nevada. Soon after takeoff, a malfunction left him with no other choice but to bail out of his airplane.

While World War II raged overseas, the United States concentrated most of its military flying training at bases in the American Southwest. LVAAF was one of the Army Air Force's primary air-to-air gunnery schools. P-39s were assigned to LVAAF beginning in 1944, and served at the base through the end of the war. In 1945, the P-39s were supplemented with Bell Aircraft's more advanced P-63 Airacobras.

One unusual squadron at the LVAAF was the "Flying Pinballs," which flew RP-63s, a modified version of a P-63. These planes were stripped of their armament and had a thicker skin added to the fuselage to protect them against dummy ammunition. Using these armored aircraft, B-17 crews had a unique opportunity to fire frangible bullets at the Airacobras, providing realistic targets in the hopes of improving the gunner's skill.

Lt. Coleman received his pilot's certificate in May 1943. By February 1945, he had accumulated nearly 300 hours of flight time, 208 of those hours in P-39s and P-63s. Coleman was assigned Bell P-39Q-20, serial number 44-3586, for his training flight on February 5, 1945. This aircraft was built at the Bell Aircraft Company's factory in Buffalo, New York, and was delivered to the Army Air Forces on February 11, 1944. On March 2, the aircraft was shipped from McClellan Army Air Field near Sacramento, California, to the Seventh Air Force in Hawaii. The aircraft was returned stateside to McClellan in August 1944, then assigned to the 3035th Base Unit (a technical

Airacobra wreckage littered the area after the aircraft exploded upon impact with the desert floor. (USAAF)

Landing gear leg and wheel rim at the crash site in 1945. (USAAF)

Then and now comparisons of the crash site looking toward the highway some 20 miles northeast of Las Vegas near Apex, Nevada.

school) at Victorville Army Air Field in Southern California the following month. P-39Q 44-3586 was transferred to the 3021st Base Unit (Flexible Gunnery School) at LVAAF, a sub-unit of the Army Air Force's Western Flying Training Command, on December 2, 1944.

Coleman's P-39 had been involved in a minor mishap on Dec. 29, 1944, when Lt. Hugh A. Wallace landed gear-up at LVAAF. A malfunction was caused by a part that prevented the landing gear from lowering. The pilot made a perfect emergency landing, damaging only the prop blades and the surface of the underbelly. The aircraft was quickly repaired and put back into service.

35

Close-up of the smoking hole where Lt. Coleman's Airacobra dove into the desert outside of Las Vegas. Somewhere below the surface lies the Bell fighter. In the foreground is the Airacobra's propeller and to the right its horizontal or vertical tail. (USAAF)

Training Flight Goes Bad

February 5 dawned clear with scattered clouds as Lt. Coleman gathered his flight information and headed out to the aircraft. After completing pre-flight inspection and starting the engine, Coleman contacted the tower and requested clearance to taxi to the runway. The tower replied, clearing the aircraft to taxi to runway twenty-two. Upon arriving at the threshold marks, Coleman was cleared to take off. Adding full power to the 1,200 hp Allison V-1710 engine, he pushed the aircraft to the required airspeed for takeoff. Seconds after liftoff, Coleman pulled the handle to retract the landing gear. As the gear came up, the left main gear indicator remained lit, signaling the wheels had not fully retracted. He immediately made several attempts to cycle the gear, but to no avail.

Out of options, he attempted to contact the tower only to discover his radio was dead. Unable to communicate with the tower, Coleman scanned his instrument panel and noticed the amperage meter indicated zero, which lead him to believe the aircraft had been running on the battery the entire time and not the generator. This indicated that an electrical short caused the aircraft's systems to run off the battery, thus draining it completely.

Wartime photo of the P-39 wreckage with Las Vegas Army Air Field crash truck and crew after having extinguished the fire. (USAAF)

    Adding to his list of problems and with no means of contacting the tower or landing the aircraft safely, Coleman decided to buzz the tower to inform them of his situation. He flew within 300 feet of the tower several times. Tower operators, unable to contact the pilot, took notice of his unusual fly-bys.

    Tower personnel quickly responded to the pilot by shooting off red flares, letting the pilot know to keep the aircraft aloft. On the ground, another P-39Q-15, serial number 44-2344, was scrambled to evaluate the problem with Coleman's aircraft.

    As the pilot of '2344 approached the crippled P-39, he radioed back to the tower the condition of Coleman's fighter. Upon visual inspection, the pilot saw that Coleman's left main gear was about one-fourth extended. As the two aircraft circled the base, several other attempts were made to lower the gear. After orbiting for a while, Coleman hand signaled the pilot of '2344 that he had approximately five gallons of fuel left in the aircraft. The pilot of '2344 radioed the tower and described the situation to the director of Training and Operations. The decision was made to have Coleman fly his fighter away from populated areas north of the base.

Approximately twenty miles north of LVAAF, Coleman jettisoned the P-39's door, rolling out onto the wing, and successfully bailing out of the stricken Airacobra. With his parachute fully opened, Coleman hung suspended in the air as he watched the aircraft wing over onto its back and dive straight into the ground, exploding upon impact. The crash occurred just 150 feet from a road, punching a hole into the side of a hill while digging a deep crater. The impact sent debris out across the desert floor.

After months of investigation, the Army Air Forces accident investigation board determined that there was not substantial evidence in the wreckage to give the exact cause of the malfunction. However, it is believed that the landing gear's manual extension crank had failed, which would have been the likely cause for the gear to operate improperly. Experienced as the pilot was, the board also felt that he had made every effort to fix the problem.

The board recommended that other measures should have been taken to save the aircraft, such as a belly landing, which may have been successful, thus giving an opportunity to investigate the malfunction and return the aircraft to service.

Examining the Crash Site

Research to locate the crash site began with a newspaper archive search and obtaining the aircraft's crash report as well as maps of the area. My father Jim, who shares my interest in finding aircraft wreck sites, and I headed for Apex, Nevada, to look for the fighter's remains.

Knowing it crashed near a road lead us to believe the chances of any substantial wreckage remaining were slim. The possibility of the road having been widened, further diminished the chances of finding the site.

Traveling on a rarely used old Nevada highway, we knew the wreckage would be at least 100 feet or more off the road. Matching the skyline with original photographs of the crash site, we knew we were in the right vicinity. The surroundings had changed little since the crash, except for the contours of a very large mountain to the north. Mining crews had blasted a large section away, altering its appearance.

Internal part with Warner Aircraft of Detroit, Michigan, data plate.

The two of us gathered our gear and decided to separate, allowing a better chance of finding the site. As we hiked to the north along the side of a hill, small fragmented pieces, reflected by the sun, could be seen. I signaled my father that I had located the wreck.

My first reaction was disappointment as I looked over the site. It appeared to be untouched, except for the litter left by motorists driving by. Trash and broken bottles had been dumped forty feet to the north and south of the impact crater. "Not much left!," my father said. My thoughts exactly. This site may not look like much, but it is part of the Las Vegas Army Air Field/Nellis Air Force Base history.

We made a number of trips to the site over a three-month period. Several interesting items were discovered on the surface in and around the impact crater. The majority of fragments found were engine block and other internal-related parts along with airframe components. Most of the aluminum fragmented pieces found were no larger than three to six inches in diameter. There were several engine valves that looked like they had been ripped, twisted, torn, and smashed, demonstrating the forces the aircraft had gone through.

Melted aluminum (slag) was discovered within the crater. Cockpit windscreen and other electronic components were also found. As the search continued, four different identification plates were discovered. Two of the plates were from an instrument while the fourth plate still had a fragmented piece attached that read: "Brake Control Unit," which could clearly be seen using a magnify glass. Probably the most unique item found was a Miles Per Hour (mph) instrument face plate, slightly twisted and bent. The gauge appeared to have only minor damage. Numbers on it could still be read more than seventy years after the crash. It is remarkable the gauge had survived laying among the harsh minerals in the soil for so long.

The crash site today is far from being encroached upon by the quick growth of the Las Vegas valley. Its remoteness may save it, but if people continue to dump trash near the site, it is possible the state may have the area cleaned up, destroying the historical site for future wreck finders.

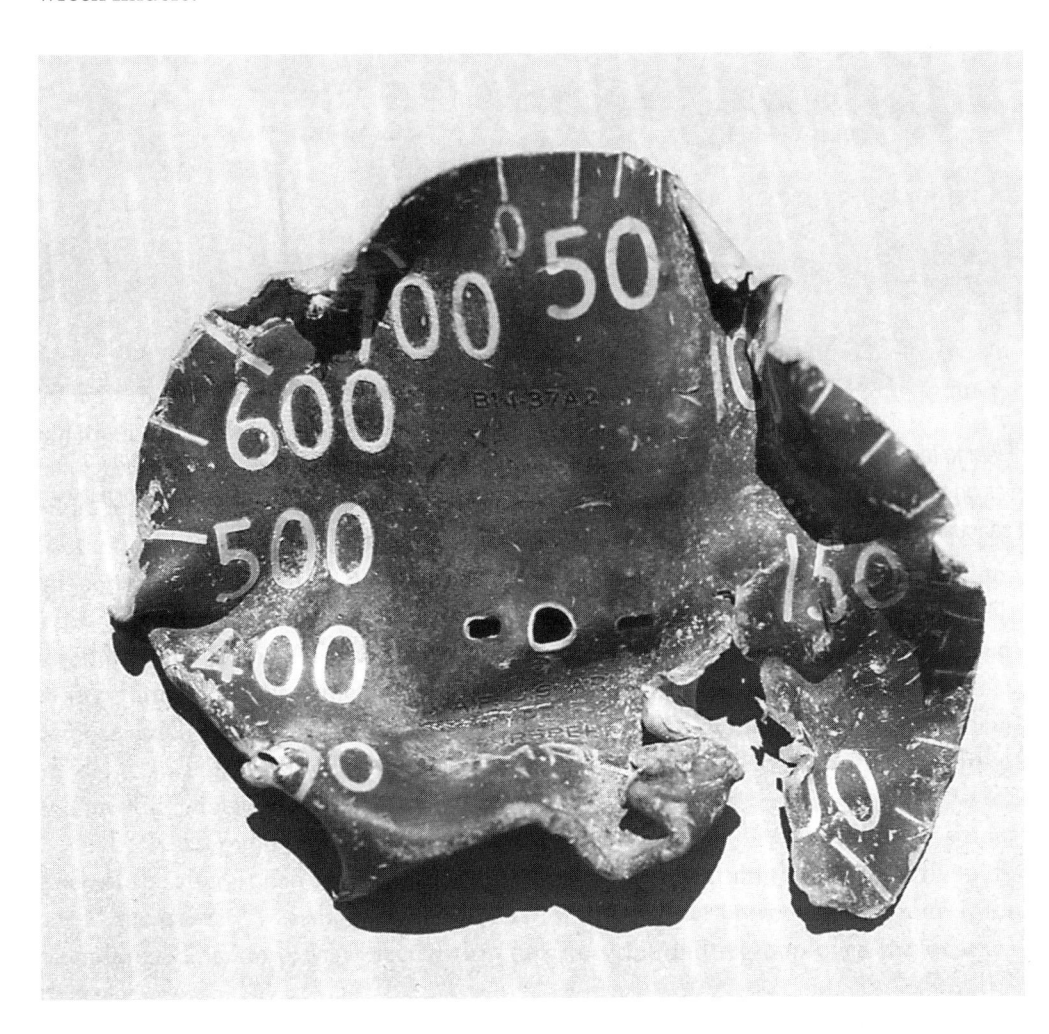

Top portion of a valve from the Airacobra's Allison engine.

Air speed indicator gauge face found at the crash site.

Two Army Planes Crash in Mid-air North of Vegas

Two army planes collided in mid-air north of Las Vegas this afternoon, according to reports received by the sheriff's office, but army officials were not able to give any information at press time.

According to members of the local police department who returned from the scene about 4 o'clock, an AT-6 collided with a B-17 bomber, both falling to earth in flames near the an Rains ranch northwest of the airport.

Army ambulances, post and city fire departments, officers from the gunnery school, sheriff's office, and police department all rushed to the scene, but were unable to get close to the burning planes which crashed about four miles apart.

The fate of the crew members could not be ascertained immediately, although some eye-witnesses reported seeing parachutes in the air.

The B-17s normally carry eight men and the AT-6 has a crew of two.

---

off was given by the tower and Westhaver and his copilot, Second Lt. Court Lake, advanced the throttles. As plumes of white smoke streamed down along the olive drab fuselage, the aircraft charged down the runway and climbed for altitude. Ascending over the Nevada desert, Westhaver's crew prepared for the mission, rechecking their equipment.

Lt. Kleiser and his group had assembled their flights in different positions around the clouds. In the second AT-6, the pilot had completed a turn getting into position approximately 500 feet behind Lt. Kleiser's aircraft when he witnessed Kleiser execute a steep turn to the left, putting him into a curving dive. Unknown to Kleiser, Westhaver's Flying Fortress had joined the formation. As Kleiser executed his gunnery curve, Westhaver's B-17 filled the AT-6's flight path. The two aircraft collided, causing a terrific explosion. Both airframes disintegrated from the impact of the midair collision, crashing in flames to the desert floor.

Many of the witnesses on the ground saw the planes collide and reported seeing parachutes floating down to earth. Aircrews from the other aircraft in the flight quickly reported the accident to the LVAAF control tower, which dispatched military emergency vehicles to the scene in hopes of finding survivors.

Upon arriving at the crash site, rescuers discovered all were killed except for one, the B-17's tail gunner Sgt. Richard Miner. He was found alive in the bomber's badly mangled tail section. This section had separated from the rest of the aircraft in the collision. With its control surfaces intact, the tail section floated down like a leaf, slowing its descent, which probably accounts for Sgt. Miner's miraculous survival. Miner was lucky enough to have only received minor bruises and a few broken bones.

Headquarters building at the Las Vegas Gunnery School located on Las Vegas Army Air Field. (USAAF)

Artist's concept of how the mid-air collision between the AT-6 and the B-17 occurred. The AT-6 punched through the bomb bay section of the Flying Fortress, dooming both crews.

Investigators found that the two descending parachutes seen by witnesses on the ground came from Kleiser's aircraft. His chute had popped open in the collision. The accident report stated that Kleiser was killed instantly when the two planes collided. As for the other parachute, it had been ejected and popped open on its own with no one strapped in. The wreckage from both planes covered a four-square-mile area.

The AT-6's engine serves as a silent memorial to the trainer's two-man crew.

Probable Cause

The findings of the investigation into the midair collision put the cause as pilot error on the part of Lt. Carlton Kleiser flying the AT-6, in that he either blacked out during his maneuver or was not looking in the direction of the B-17. The contributory cause was Lt. Donald Westhaver in the B-17G. His aircraft was not part of the gunnery exercise, and the exercise group probably did not see the B-17 approaching from the rear. The Army Air Forces recommended that a more careful study of scheduling of missions be made, so that aircraft in the same flight can take off together. It was further recommended that no pilot ever join another formation unannounced.

Finding the B-17's Crash Site

The wreckage of the B-17 and the AT-6 lay scattered across the Nevada desert, twenty miles north of Las Vegas and fifteen miles northwest of Las Vegas Army Air Field, today Nellis Air Force Base. While having access to the history office at the base and assisting them with wrecks in the area, I had the opportunity to troll through hundreds of photos in their library. Finding the images of the B-17/AT-6 midair,

The B-17's starboard horizontal and elevator point awkwardly skyward. Compare the hills in the background of this photo with the contemporary image taken at the crash site. Aside from a line of utility wires and poles, not much has changed in this area of the desert outside Las Vegas.

I submitted for the crash report and the research began. Using a quad-map and the Air Force accident report photos to triangulate the mountains shown in the images, the approximate location of the crash site was determined and the coordinates entered into GPS. This set up a two- to three-square mile search area. Also aiding in the search were four black-and-white photos obtained from the base historian. These would be used to match the terrain to narrow down the search area.

Driving to the site, a few stops were made to match the photos with the GPS coordinates. The photo of the tail section laying on its side was most helpful as it showed the line of mountains in the background. Once the general area was determined, I began to search on foot. Seeing that houses had recently been built in the area was not a positive sign as the crash site had the potential of resting in someone's backyard.

After hiking along the desert, what appeared to be a shut-off valve of some kind was spotted. It was a good sign, but not proof of a B-17 or an AT-6 part as the military had used this area for years and it could have come from a variety of vehicles. A few scattered fragments were found, then a large concentration of wreckage came into view. Upon closer examination, it was determined to be the cockpit area of the B-17. Instrument housings and gauge inserts were rapidly uncovered. A map light was found along with one of two oil pressure gauges used on the B-17. The gauge was less than 25 percent visible above ground. The desert's harsh mineral-rich soil had eaten away at the aluminum instrument face.

Author Doug Scroggins sorts through various small components from the mid-air collision. The mineral-rich soil combined with desert rain storms will soon make these aircraft parts unrecognizable.

One of the 16mm combat camera film magazines was discovered on the fourth sweep of the area. The extent of the corrosion is easily discernable.

A second visit to the crash site was made. This time the author's father, J.D. Scroggins, joined the search, which began at the B-17 cockpit's point of impact and was the starting point for finding the bomber's other sections.

It was known that the debris covered a large area and the search started to the north to cover a one-half-mile area. No more than fifteen minutes into the hike, a darkened patch was seen on the desert floor. Close examination revealed fragments that belonged to one of the B-17's engines. Soon after, just south of the B-17 cockpit area, another burned, dark patch was discovered. After spending hours hiking and searching, a most unusual item was found-a flare gun. If it wasn't for the brush that hid it all these years, the gun could have been severely damaged by off-road traffic.

A third trip was made to the site a few months later. On that afternoon, one of the gun camera's film magazines was located.

Research into the crash site is ongoing and will be for many years. However, the relics from this midair collision may be lost forever. New homes and freeway expansion projects will soon be moving into the area and will claim this land.

One of the B-17's oil pressure gauges survived the crash, only to suffer the effects of the post-crash fire.

The B-17s flare gun sat undisturbed under the Nevada brush for more than 50 years.

AT-6D similar to the pair of Luke Army Air Field aircraft that went missing in March 1945. The Luke aircraft were identified by the base letter 'X' and the buzz number in large lettering on both sides of the fuselage. (Photo by Roland Muth)

Chapter 5

Luke Field Missions: A Trio of AT-6s Go Missing

Craig Fuller

Sub Lt. Shao-chang Van was a Chinese Air Force Air Cadet training at Luke Army Air Field outside of Phoenix, Ariz. It was March 14, 1945, about 7:30 p.m. Mountain War Time (MWT) as he walked on the ramp toward his assigned airplane. It was ship number X-330 of the 8th Squadron at Luke Field. X-330 was an AT-6D, serial number 42-85684, manufactured at the North American Aviation plant in Dallas, Texas. This particular aircraft, 42-85684, had been accepted by the U.S. Army Air Forces on Aug. 18, 1944, and, by the time of Sub. Lt. Van's flight, had accumulated a little more than 650 hours on its airframe.

Sub Lt. Van had so far built up a little more than 400 hours of flight experience. He started primary training in Glendale, Arizona, in February 1944, went on to Marana Army Air Field (AAF) for basic training in April of that year, and then transferred to Luke in July for advanced training. He was now in the Instructors School at Luke. He planned to become an instructor, then return to China so he could train Chinese pilots to help in the Allied effort in the Pacific Theater.

On March 14, 1945, Sub Lt. Van was going to fly a solo cross-country from Luke to Yuma AAF, then to Blythe AAF in California, with the return leg back to Luke Field. He had flown this cross-county three times before – once before at night, and once in daylight in an AT-6 while he was doing his cadet training at Luke. The third time was in a P-40 gunnery trainer from Luke. That was an exhilarating experience for him. While the P-40 was no longer one of the hottest fighters at this point in the war, it definitely had a lot more performance than the AT-6. Having spent the last two years hearing stories of the Flying Tigers flying P-40s defending his homeland and

49

Page one of the accident report for 24-year old Sub Lt. Saho-chang Van, a Chinese pilot being trained at Luke Field, Arizona. Van had accumulated 262.25 hours of flight time as pilot in command, with a little more than 400 hours in the air. (Craig Fuller Collection)

also having the six 0.50-cal. machine guns in the wing instead of just two forward firing 0.30-cal. guns helped make his adrenaline flow on that trip.

However, on this evening his flight would be in an AT-6, like what he would be flying at home to train Chinese students. He took off from Luke at 8:14 p.m. MWT and headed off into the night.

Sub Lt. Shao-chang Van was declared overdue at 10:45 p.m., when he failed to return. He was not heard from again.

On the morning of March 15, Luke Field initiated a search for Sub Lt. Shao-chang Van without any luck. The next day, the Second Air Force Search and Rescue Unit was notified that X-330 and another Luke AT-6, X-415, were missing. The second AT-6 was on a routine training flight when it disappeared, again with no radio contact. The Second Air Force search command aircraft, a C-46, was in Deming, New Mexico, at the time and its pilot, Lt. Gore, was instructed to proceed immediately to Phoenix. Upon arriving at Phoenix, Lt. Gore picked up the Civil Air Patrol operations officer and they proceeded to Yuma AAF.

And yet again, later in the day, a third AT-6 disappeared while searching for the previous two aircraft.

On March 17, four Civil Air Patrol aircraft searched Southwestern Arizona for a combined total of 30 hours. Additionally, 10 Yuma AAF BT-13s searched California and Arizona for a combined total of 130 hours, but still Sub Lt. Shao-chang Van's aircraft was not found.

On March 18, the four Civil Air Patrol aircraft took off for Ajo, Ariz., to search that area until sundown, when they were to return to Phoenix. Still no luck.

Sub Lt. Shao-chang Van's AT-6D X-330 (42-85684) was found four days after it went down at the base of Big Horn Peak, 45-miles west of Phoenix. Photo from the crash report is seen to the right, and indicates where the wing impacted and the tail came to rest. Compare the report photo to the photo of the crash site today at left. (Craig Fuller, left; U.S. Army Air Force via Craig Fuller, right)

Debris field of Sub Lt. Shao-chang Van's AT-6D X330. In the top photo the aircraft's buzz number can be seen as well as the national insignia. The aircraft's data block is seen in the lower image. (Craig Fuller photos)

Luke-based AT-6D X-415 was not located until May 5, 1945, after the snow had melted in the area. The photo above shows the aircraft's wing and fuel tank, while the engine cylinders, fuselage skin, and a radio can be seen in the brush in the photo below. (Craig Fuller Photos)

By the end of the day on March 19, the ten BT-13s from Yuma had completed their search of Arizona and California, and the Mexican government was contacted for permission to expand the search into Mexico. The request was granted and on March 20, the C-46 search command aircraft, six BT-13s, and one AT-11 searched in Mexico for a combined total of 20 hours. That evening an AT-6 from Luke flew out to investigate a lead that someone had spotted what looked like aircraft wreckage at the base of Big Horn Peak, 45-miles west of Phoenix. As the pilot flew over the crash site he was able to establish that it was indeed an AT-6 crash, but it would have to wait until the next day for a ground crew to positively identify the particular aircraft and determine which of the three missing AT-6s it was, or if it was from one of the many previous accidents that littered the desert.

Upon arriving at the AT-6 wreckage on March 21, investigators found that the aircraft had struck the ground with considerable force. The left wing had hit first, followed immediately by the engine, which dug a hole five feet in diameter. The rest of the wreckage was in a straight line strewn across 70 yards. One of the propeller blades was sticking out of the hole dug by the engine, and the rest of the engine was eight yards past that. The right wing and tail assembly had been thrown 38 yards from the impact point, with the center section being the furthest at 70 yards. Small pieces were scattered on either side along the same line as the main wreckage. The wreck was at the head of a box canyon on a gentle slope heading west. A side panel was found with the serial number of the aircraft, it was 42-85684, which confirmed it was Sub Lt. Shao-chang Van's plane. He had been killed instantly in the crash.

The search had continued in Mexico that day until those searchers were notified of the find. A total of 183 hours were flown by 16 aircraft in the search for Sub Lt. Shao-chang Van's plane.

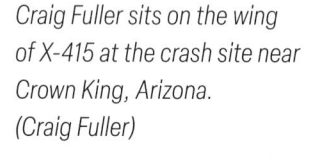

Craig Fuller sits on the wing of X-415 at the crash site near Crown King, Arizona. (Craig Fuller)

The search for the second AT-6, X-415, was abandoned after 750 hours had been flown. X-415 was not found until late spring when the snow had melted enough to expose the aircraft on a mountainside. The third AT-6, X-128, got caught in a down-draft and crashed near the top of a mountain saddle. Both crewmembers survived the crash and after spending the day by the plane hiked to an abandoned cabin where they spent the night. The following morning the crew hiked into the town of Crown King and reported their crash. Unknown at the time, two crewmembers had crashed within ten miles of the second missing AT-6, X-415. Of interest, in March 1944, three more Luke AT-6s had crashed within a few miles of where X-415 and X-128 had come to rest. During the Korean War, in September 1952, a Luke F-84 crashed within two miles of X-415.

Today most of the wreckage of X-330 is still at the base of Big Horn Peak. Some of the larger pieces have since been removed and the remaining wreckage was broken up and covered with rocks and brush to help make it less visible from the air. The impact crater from the engine is still visible, and the side panel with the serial number and Luke Field stenciled onto it can also be found. Large pieces of both wings remain at the site. One wing has 864 (the last three numbers of the serial number) and the other has the national insignia still visible on it. Despite being within view of a major highway, X-330's location being on the opposite side of a canal and in a wilderness area has made it almost forgotten except to the occasional hiker crossing the desert.

AT-6D X-415's engine mount, firewall, and tube frame at the crash site. (Craig Fuller)

PB4Y-2 Buno. 59554, flown by a civilian crew from Consolidated Vultee Aircraft, lost their lives when factory workers failed to install 98 bolts holding on the left outer wing panel. Installation of the missing bolts was signed off by an inspector. (U.S. Navy/National Archives)

Chapter 6

Failure at the Factory: Convair Plant Mishaps

Nicholas A. Veronico

In 1944, San Diego, California, was a town filled with the hustle and bustle of people working in the war industries along with soldiers, sailors, and Marines on shore leave. There was a constant drone of new aircraft flying overhead. While civilians worked around the clock shifts at the Consolidated Vultee aircraft factory at Lindbergh Field – the city's airport situated between downtown and Point Loma – military fliers from nearby Camp Kearny, Brown Field, and Naval Air Station North Island flew search patrols and training missions.

During the war, the Consolidated Vultee factory at Lindbergh Field built PBY Catalina flying boats, four-engine B-24 Liberator bombers, PB4Y-2 Privateer patrol planes, and began production of the U.S. Army Air Forces' four-engine B-32 Dominator (designed to supplement the Boeing's B-29 Superfortress).

Consolidated Vultee's PB4Y-2 Privateer was a modification of the company's successful B-24 bomber in use by the United States Navy. The fuselage of the –2 was lengthened seven feet to accommodate a radar operator's station and was fitted with two upper turrets, two side blister turrets, and a nose turret. The side and nose turrets could traverse to fire under the aircraft, negating the need for a ball turret. Used primarily against Japanese shipping, the aircraft was deployed to the Pacific Theater in January 1945. Privateers had a wingspan of 110 feet, a length of 74 feet, 7 inches, and was 30 feet tall at the tip of the tail. The PB4Y-2 had a top speed of 237 mph at 13,750 feet, a service ceiling of 20,700 feet, and a maximum range of 2,800 miles. Empty, the plane weighed 37,485 pounds and had a gross weight of 65,000 pounds. Its role as an anti-shipping patrol bomber mandated that the engines be fitted with single stage, two-speed superchargers for better performance between sea level and 10,000

Aerial view showing San Diego Bay, Lindbergh Field, the flight path of BuNo 59544, the location of the wing, and the aircraft's final resting place. (U.S. Navy/National Archives)

feet. In all, Consolidated Vultee delivered 739 PB4Y-2s and thirty-three cargo versions designated RY-3s (Liberator Mk. IX).

Three incidents during Privateer construction, each within a six-month time span – two in the same month – were preventable. These incidents illustrate the failure of some process or chain of events at the factory, which could have prevented the loss of aircraft and six lives.

Missing Wing Bolts

The sun shone brightly on November 22, 1944, as PB4Y-2 Bureau of Aeronautics serial number (Buno.) 59544 sat on the ramp at Lindbergh Field ready for its maiden flight. After rolling off the Consolidated Vultee production line, an aircraft's first flight was flown by a company crew. If there were no squawks, the aircraft was presented to the Navy's Bureau of Aeronautics Representative (BAR) for its acceptance flight. Then, if the BAR was satisfied, the aircraft was accepted and subsequently flown from the Consolidated Vultee factory in San Diego to the Navy's modification line at Litchfield Park, outside of Phoenix, Arizona, for installation of the nose turret and other government furnished equipment and modifications needed to make the plane combat ready.

At 10 a.m., Consolidated Vultee's Inspection Department noted that the aircraft had 1,800 gallons of fuel in its four main tanks, and certified that the aircraft was ready

EXHIBIT "I"

The PB4Y-2 plane crash was probably the biggest thing to happen in the quiet Loma Portal neighborhood then and now. The port outer wing panel's size can be determined when comparing it to the height of the men standing around it. Notice the vacant lot next door. (U.S. Navy/National Archives)

Compare this photograph with the 1944 photo of 3121 Kingsley St. Other than the removal of some bushes near the front of the lawn and the two shrubs against the front of the house, as well as the growth of three palm trees, everything looks the same. (Nicholas A. Veronico)

Scene of the crash showing the short distance between where the detached wing panel landed and the crash site. The area of the crash has since been built up with houses. (U.S. Navy/National Archives)

for its first flight. The company crew arrived at the aircraft around 11:30 a.m., and began the preflight inspection and systems check. The crew of six consisted of Pilot Marvin R. Weller, Copilot Conrad C. Cappe, Flight Engineers Frank D. Sands and Clifford P. Bengston, Radio Operator Robert B. Skala, and Consolidated Vultee field operations employee Ray Estes.

Weller and Cappe taxied Buno. 59544 to the end of the runway, which parallels San Diego Bay. Applying full power, the Privateer's four 1,350-horsepower Pratt & Whitney R-1830-94 engines roared to life. As 59544 picked up speed, Weller and Cappe lifted the aircraft off the runway. Climbing for altitude, the pilots heard a loud crack as the port outer wing panel tore away. The loss of the wing panel caused an asymmetric lift condition from which the pilots could not recover.

The port outer wing panel was described to have "twisted like a leaf," striking the roof of the front bedroom of the home at 3121 Kingsley St. in the Loma Portal neighborhood near the airfield. The wing panel came to rest on the lawn. The single-story residence was owned by Cmdr. A.B. Cartwright, and, at the time of the accident, his wife was in the backyard watching the whole incident unfold. House guests of the Cartwrights were inside the home, but they were not injured. It was now 12:23 p.m.

With the port outer wing panel gone, the remainder of the aircraft began to lose what little altitude it had. The massive four-engine patrol bomber continued another one-quarter mile before striking a ravine in an undeveloped section of Loma Portal, near the Navy Training Center. The aircraft had traveled less than two miles from the point of lift-off. San Diego City firemen and military rescue crews raced to the scene, only to find the aircraft engulfed in flames and the crew of six dead.

In the aftermath of the crash, the wreckage was hauled away for inspection. Two days later, on November 24, Consolidated Vultee officials announced that four employees (C.R. Alexander, H.B. Hendryz, J.E. Lahyer, and J.C. Hedgpeth) were terminated. They were directly responsible for either installing bolts that connected the outer wing panel to the wing center section, or they were inspectors who had signed off the work (none of which had been done). Although the four spar bolts had held the wing panel were in place, a post-crash inspection revealed that ninety-eight additional bolts were missing and never installed. Navy officials immediately ordered an inspection of the wing panel attach points of all PB4Y-2 aircraft in service.

On the human side, each of the families was compensated an average of $21,000 for the loss of their loved one. This included $10,000 in aviation accident insurance, group insurance death benefits, any retirement annuity from the company, and a one-time payment of $6,000 from California's Workers Compensation fund. In all, $130,484.86 was paid to the families of the six crewmen.

On January 5, 1945, a San Diego coroner's jury voted 11-1 to find Consolidated Vultee guilty of "gross negligence" in the six deaths. Subsequently, on December 4, 1945, the Bureau of Aeronautics reduced the number of aircraft deliverable on the contract by one to 739, and reduced the amount paid to Consolidated Vultee by $155,000.

PB4Y-2 Buno. 59554, flown by a civilian crew from Consolidated Vultee Aircraft, lost their lives when factory workers failed to install 98 bolts holding on the left outer wing panel. Installation of the missing bolts was signed off by an inspector. (U.S. Navy/National Archives)

After recovery from in front of the Kingsley Street home, the left outer wing panel was thoroughly examined. It was quickly determined that workers failed to connect the panel by omitting 98 bolts. Only the four spar attach bolts were installed, having failed shortly after takeoff. (U.S. Navy/National Archives)

At the crash site of PB4Y-2 Buno. 59544, parts of the giant patrol bomber can still be found just under the surface. (Nicholas A. Veronico)

59544: The Crash Site Today

As time passes, memories fade of that long ago day when a Consolidated Vultee PB4Y-2 fell out of the sky at Point Loma. Through many a paint job and a potential remodel or two, 3121 Kingsley St. has maintained its 1930's classic California charm.

At the impact site of Buno. 59554, Navy crews worked to rescue any possible survivors. Notice the hole chopped into the rear fuselage near the horizontal stabilizer. 'A' denotes the unusual shoulder of the hill, and 'B' shows the starboard outer wing panel laying across a drainage ditch. (U.S. Navy/National Archives)

The crash site today: 'A' is the shoulder of the hill leading up to Oleander Drive. The Navy barracks were located behind this hill. 'B' shows the drainage ditch, and 'C' marks an area where debris from the crash was found 60 years after the event.

The first sign of trouble: Smoke rises above the factories around Lindbergh Field as Buno. 59836 becomes fully engulfed in flames. (U.S. Coast Guard/Platnick via Todd Hackbarth)

A Ryan Fireball lost a wing and the resulting wreckage dropped onto PB4Y-2 Buno. 59836 as it sat on the Lindbergh Field ramp. Ryan immediately added a skin doubler to the wing, and looked at reengineering the canopy release latch. (U.S. Navy)

Today, the exterior of the home is little changed from that November 1944 day when an aircraft's outer wing panel impacted the roof. The lawn is tightly manicured and a rich green color, and the shutters that framed the front bedroom window are still in place. The porch's lathe-turned support post remains the same. During the intervening decades since the crash, three palm trees were planted and have matured. Kingsley Street is peaceful and has changed little since the war.

The main impact point, however, is a different story. Houses have sprung up, hiding the terrain and masking the Privateer's final resting place. Drawing a line up Kingsley St. and moving left 10 degrees puts the aircraft crash site in a ravine bordered by Oleander Dr. and Larga Cir. on the north and east, and Azalea Dr. and Wisteria Dr. on the west and south. Interestingly, the houses that border this area all share a common area behind their backyards. Each borders this canyon, with the impact site at the bottom of the ravine. Note that there is no public access to this area, and it is private property belonging to the surrounding homeowners.

Comparing the crash scene photographs to the site today, one can still see the drainage ditch at the bottom of the ravine and the shoulder-shaped hill below the homes. To the east, the Navy barracks are gone, replaced by homes and a Home Depot store in the distance.

In the ravine, a close examination of the ground yields pieces that were once molten aluminum, sections of Fiberglas insulation, plexiglass, and other small parts. It is also the ground where Consolidated Vultee employees Marvin R. Weller, Conrad C. Cappe, Frank D. Sands, Clifford P. Bengston, Robert B. Skala, and Ray Estes gave their lives in service of their country. Their sacrifice will not be forgotten.

Freak Accident

The morning of April 5, 1945, was another fine San Diego day. Lt. D.W. Rietz had accepted PB4Y-2 Buno. 59836 from the Bureau of Aeronautics Representative for delivery to the modification line at Litchfield Park. At 10:45 a.m., Rietz sent the enlisted crew, Aviation Machinists Mates G.R. Brown and J.H. Randall, out to the plane with everyone's flight gear. Ten minutes later, Rietz and Lt. J.E. Creed climbed aboard the Privateer and settled in, beginning to work through the checklists.

Also located on Lindbergh Field was Ryan Aeronautical Co. At 11:00 a.m., Dean Lake, a Ryan test pilot, was flying an experimental XFR-1 "Fireball," Buno. 48234, over the field. The Fireball was powered by a Wright R-1820-56 piston engine and featured a General Electric J31-GE turbojet engine that took air in at the wing roots and produced thrust through a tailpipe at the rear of the fuselage. The FR-1 was described as having "One turning, and one burning."

As Lake crossed above Lindbergh Field, the skin between the front and rear spars on the right wing tore off and the airflow over the open hole caused the wing to disintegrate. A second plausible theory claims the canopy departed in flight and knocked off the tail.

With the wing folding up, Lake jumped from the aircraft and parachuted to safety. As Lake floated down, his FR-1 tore itself to pieces. Momentum carried the craft further, spinning over Lindbergh Field and crashing into the fuselage of the Privateer occupied by Lt. Rietz and his crew. Rietz, Creed, and Brown were able to exit the aircraft without injuries. Randall was not so lucky. He suffered first, second, and third degree burns as well as mild lacerations.

Both aircraft were completely destroyed.

Sailors, Coast Guardsmen, and factory workers try to extinguish the flames of 59836 after a Ryan Fireball crashed into it. Four of the PB4Y-2's crew escaped, one with serious injuries. (U.S. Coast Guard/Platnick via Todd Hackbarth)

When an unqualified mechanic attempted to remove a battery solenoid, he broke an hydraulic line. The subsequent fluid spill ignited with the results shown here. Buno. 59350, the first production PB4Y-2 and was completely destroyed. (U.S. Navy/National Archives)

To address the accident's probable cause, Ryan Aeronautical added a .064-inch skin doubler between the wing spars, and experimented with a new canopy and canopy release mechanism in tests in the 40-foot-by-80-foot wind tunnel at the National Advisory Committee for Aeronautics' (NACA, the forerunner of today's NASA) Ames Aeronautical Laboratory in Mountain View, California.

Qualified Personnel Required

In the late evening of April 30, 1945, the first production PB4Y-2, Buno. 59350, was on the Lindbergh Field ramp being prepared for a flight to Naval Air Station Minneapolis, Minnesota. At the time, Consolidated Vultee's midnight shift change was taking place. Mechanic Milton H. Fisher was instructed by Crew Chief Charles Zimmerman to remove the port battery solenoid, which is located fourteen inches below the cockpit floor. At 11:59 p.m. local time, Fisher was attempting to remove the nut that attaches the positive battery cable to the solenoid.

Fisher, not a trained electrician, had begun working without disconnecting the battery. Three inches above the nut were a series of hydraulic lines. As Fisher rotated the socket's rachet handle, it punctured a hydraulic line sending fluid over the battery and solenoid. The fluid ignited, and when help arrived Fisher was found outside the aircraft with severe burns. The entire aircraft burned, with only the number four engine considered salvageable.

The cause of the fire was officially listed as: "due to the assignment of a mechanic to perform electrical work which should be attempted only by a qualified electrician; an electrical short circuit between the battery terminal of the port battery solenoid and the adjacent hydraulic line. This condition resulted when [an] employee attempted to disconnect the positive battery cable terminal, at the solenoid, with a metal wrench without disconnecting the battery."

Safety First

Whether it is a design flaw or human error, in each of the above accidents the aircraft was a total loss. In one case, six people lost their lives. These three incidents, although of varying causes, illustrate the need to establish or follow procedures, and approach each task with an eye to safety.

PB4Y-2 Buno. 59350 is seen progressing down Consolidated Aircraft's San Diego production line in 1944. Buno. 59350 was the first of 740 Privateers built, although only 739 were delivered to the Navy with the loss of Buno. 59544 while being flown by a Consolidated Aircraft crew. (U.S. Navy via National Archives)

The aft section of Navy R4D Bureau number 17228 rests on a hillside in San Carlos, California, on the morning of March 15, 1945. The transport had crashed during a heavy storm the night before, and was off course by fifteen miles to the southwest when it impacted the coastal foothills of the San Francisco Peninsula. (U.S. Navy photo)

Chapter 7

Sixteen Survive Navy Transport Crash in San Carlos, California

Nicholas A. Veronico and Jeff Christner

Low ceilings, rain, worsening weather, loss of situational awareness in relation to the airfield, and rising terrain conspired to bring an end to a Navy R4D attempting to land in the San Francisco Bay area on March 14, 1945. The transport, a military version of the Douglas DC-3, was carrying a crew of three and twenty passengers and was en route from San Pedro in Southern California to Oakland that night. Seven servicemen perished when the transport impacted the hills behind the city of San Carlos, halfway between San Francisco and San Jose, on the peninsula side of the bay.

That evening there was a rain storm with clouds reported as low as 1,000 feet and visibility of only three miles. As the R4D transport flew north toward Oakland, the weather closed in and the cloud ceilings dropped to 500 feet, but this updated information was not passed to the pilots. Unsuccessful at landing during their first attempt at Oakland, the pilots chose to go-around and try again. They followed the "missed-approach" procedure for the airport, turning to the west and circling around for another approach. In the storm, the flight crew seems to have become lost in the clouds above the bay and were now flying more than fifteen miles to the south and west of Oakland Airport.

This Navy R4D, Buno. number 17096, is a sister-ship to the one that crashed in the hills of San Carlos. The R4D is the Navy version of the Douglas DC-3 airliner. (Ed Davies Collection)

At 8:12 p.m., the Navy transport, R4D-5 Bureau of Aeronautics serial number 17228, impacted the San Carlos hills at an altitude of 630 feet. Of the twenty-three on board, the three-member crew were killed along with four servicemen sitting in the forward passenger cabin while the remaining sixteen passengers survived with various degrees of injury. Killed were pilot Lt. (j.g.) William Karlick, copilot Ens. Clois Holmes Jr., and flight orderly Robert A. Trout, along with passengers LCdr. Robert H. Allen, LCdr. John Brahtz, as well as Richard Johnston and Victor Salazar Jr., both seamen first class.

One of the Navy crash survivors was eighteen-year-old Seaman First Class Ralph W. Sedlack. He had joined the sea service in late 1944 and graduated from the Quartermaster School at the U.S. Naval Training Center at Sampson, New York, less than a month before the R4D came to grief. From his training station in New York, he was assigned to the Pacific Theater of Operations. Traveling from the East Coast, Sedlack flew to Kansas, followed by San Diego on the West Coast, before heading north to Oakland, California, which would be his port of embarkation. From Oakland, he would head to his initial assignment in the Pacific Theater. Sedlack's journey was interrupted by the crash and the night's rainy weather assured his survival. Having suffered a broken back, he would not have been able to extricate himself from the wreckage had there been a post-crash fire. The lack of fire and the rainy weather gave time for the rescue crews to reach the stricken R4D and triage the injured.

STORM BLAMED IN PLANE CRASH

7 Dead, 16 Injured as Navy Craft Cracks Up Near San Carlos

Seven men died and sixteen others suffered injuries when a Navy transport plane smashed itself against a fog shrouded hillside west of San Carlos on

After crash survivor Ralph W. Sedlack had healed, he served aboard three ships, starting with the destroyer USS Wickes *(DD-578), followed by the destroyer escorts USS* Dennis *(DE-405), and USS* Richard S. Bull *(DE-402). He served as a Quartermaster, third class. After the war he attended New York University and Stevens University in New Jersey where he earned electrical engineering degrees. (Courtesy Charlanne and Hal Brown)*

Sailors and airmen from the naval station at Tanforan and Treasure Island joined with local volunteer firefighters to extract the survivors from the plane wreckage. The terrain was steep, slippery, and muddy as the men worked during the raging winter storm. (U.S. Navy photo)

Researching the R4D Crash

Beginning with newspaper accounts of the time, it was reported that Charles L. Gracy, a guard at the former San Carlos War Dog Training Center, heard the transport fly over, very low, followed by the terrific sound of the aircraft impacting the hill. Gracy phoned the San Carlos Police, and Chief Edward J. Wheeler and Patrolman Russell Rodgers responded to the scene. Soon after, sixteen ambulances arrived to take the injured to nearby San Mateo County General Hospital and Dibble Army Hospital in Menlo Park. Local volunteer firefighters and sailors from the base at Tanforan in San Bruno and Treasure Island came to help in the rescue. Of the sixteen men that survived the crash, most suffered serious injuries, but they had survived.

The author asked around town as to the location of the Dog Training Center, but this was a temporary dead end as, at the time, no one could pinpoint the base. The late aviation historian William "Bill" Carpentier was able to aid in the search as he was stationed at the San Carlos War Dog Training Center, officially known as the Western Remount Area Reception and Training Center, where he trained to take a dog to the Pacific Theater. Carpentier sent a map outlining the War Dog Training Center showing that the Army camp was on the former H&H Ranch property adjacent to the former Devonshire Country Club clubhouse at the top of Club Drive. During the war, more than 2,500 military dog handlers and 4,500 dogs were trained at the facility, so it was no small place. Many of the men were billeted at the Devonshire Country Club.

Navy personnel inspect the wreckage of R4D 17228. The radio operator or navigator's chair can be seen in the right foreground on top of the left wing panel. (U.S. Navy photo)

how the hill looks today. Changing my sight picture, I realized that if the foreground hill had been graded during home construction, even though the hills and gullies might look similar, the hill would now appear smaller or shorter if it was graded down, making us want to search closer or lower in elevation than we normally would. I then threw the aviation archaeology book out the window and completely discounted finding the crash site by lining up the hills. There had to be another way.

One technique we had used in the past was locating search areas using trees visible in old aircraft accident photographs. We would find a tree in an old photo, preferably one with aircraft debris nearby, and we would then try to match up historic aerial imagery taken around the time of the crash to find that same tree. Google Earth works well in this endeavor since one can then switch the view to current aerial imagery. This will offer a good idea of what the location looks like now and help define a search area. We jokingly termed this technique "treesearching," since it rhymed with researching, and often we would get fairly accurate locations of remaining debris from a crash using this method.

Looking from above the wreckage to the next hilltop and into the San Francisco Bay. Like many accidents, had the aircraft been another 200 feet higher, it would have missed the coastal hills completely and most likely made a safe landing at its intended destination. (U.S. Navy photo)

Wreckage of the Navy R4D transport plane that crashed in the hills of San Carlos on March 14, 1945, is examined by local authorities in the days following the accident. This crash took the lives of seven servicemen. This photo and others shot the same day helped researchers locate the crash site more than 75 years after the accident. There is now an interpretive plaque at the entrance to Big Canyon Park to remember the sacrifices made by these men. (Author's Collection)

Shot from the backyard of a home on Regent Court above the crash site, this view shows the contour lines of the hills and canyons that enabled searchers to located the Navy transport's final resting place. (Nicholas A. Veronico)

We had taken some bearings using this technique before, but only so much as to say that a piece came to rest approximately fifty feet south of a tree seen in an old aircraft accident photo. If the old tree was removed, either by development, or as a result of recovering the aircraft, at least one could get decent GPS coordinates of where it was and search from there. All this depends on matching up the right trees, which when done successfully, not only leads to the search area, but also gives hints as to the location where the crash report or news photographs were taken. We used this technique extensively in our search of the Flying Tiger Line Flight 282 crash site (see *Wreckchasing 101* – Chapter 15 for more information on that accident).

I decided to use our treesearching technique to get a bearing from the R4D-5 crash report photo. The background hill has a peak, one that exists today, that we could use to line up with trees on the foreground hill as seen in the crash report photo. Thankfully, there were quite a few trees on that foreground hill and after some careful comparison of the crash report photo and aerial imagery from 1948, I was able to get a bearing from that background hill between two trees visible on the crash report photo. I then transposed that heading onto current aerial imagery to form a search line. Our search along the line would be somewhat limited given that we would still use the foreground hill in the crash report photo, but only as a general guide. Too close to the hill along the search line threw the image way off, too far back along the search line and we would be inside someone's house or standing in the middle of the street. We were happy to see that a large portion of the search line was in the open space area behind people's houses.

Using our search line as a guide, we hiked into the open space and began exploring. The line went through an area heavily covered by manzanita bushes, thorn bushes, low lying trees, and growing up through it all, poison oak. If that wasn't bad enough, the soil on the steep hillsides was loose and we had to fight for every step up or down. One thing I noticed on the 1948 aerial imagery was a gulley. I had originally suspected that maybe it was carved by a bulldozer, tractor, or whatever had been used to remove the wreckage in 1945. The gulley still existed in the open space and the search line went

Researchers Jeff Christner and his son Paxton were able to locate pieces of the Navy transport among the brush in Big Canyon Park confirming the aircraft's final resting place. (Courtesy Jeff Christner)

right through it. Now I know that any line drawn between points on historic aerial imagery using trees won't be 100 percent accurate, especially when drawing that same search line on a crash report photo taken from the ground. However, we were lucky in two regards. One, the historic aerial imagery of San Carlos was taken only three years after the crash in 1948, so the trees wouldn't have changed that much. And two, since the R4D-5 crashed perpendicular to the search line, that is at a 90-degree angle to it, provided part of it was in the open space area and not under homes or streets, there should still be something left to find. Given all this I felt a one- or two-degree error in our bearing would still put us on the right track.

As we were searching the steep gulley, my heart literally skipped a beat. Right on the surface was something that immediately looked like aircraft debris, and not household debris. It was round, obviously aluminum, was painted light gray, and had a connector on the back. After photographing it in place, I turned it over, revealing a blue lens with a unique sawtooth pattern. The bracket was aluminum and the piece had a unique screw hole pattern that I felt could be tracked down. It was not until we returned home that I was able to identify this piece. The unique screw hole and sawtooth pattern on the lens matched perfectly to a map or cabin light, possibly made by Grimes Manufacturing, and the only use of this item I could find was on aircraft. Grimes Manufacturing used ink stamps on their lights, so whatever markings were applied at the factory were now covered by the gray paint. This was the first piece found from the R4D-5 and it was found less than fifteen feet off the search line we plotted. We also located a few other suspect items, but nothing that could be confirmed as coming from an aircraft. This one find confirmed our treesearching technique and only whetted our appetite to find more of the aircraft.

A group of friends interested in locating the crash site of Navy R4D-5 Buno. 17228 gathered on a warm Saturday to search Big Canyon Park for remnants of the World War II transport's crash site. The plane's final resting place was located on a subsequent hike. (Nicholas A. Veronico)

Researchers Jeff Christner and his son Paxton were able to locate pieces of the Navy transport among the brush in Big Canyon Park confirming the aircraft's final resting place. (Courtesy Jeff Christner)

A week later, my son and I again headed to San Carlos to search for anything else we could find from the R4D-5 crash. After finding the map or cabin light the previous weekend, I decided to do additional treesearching to try to get multiple bearings using trees in the crash report photo compared to the trees in the historic aerial imagery. I figured three bearings would be good enough to put us close to the actual crash site and after plotting these lines on Google Earth and tilting the view downward, the Google Earth image looked just like the crash report photo. The three bearing lines intersected just west of a wooded area, which closely matched the background in the crash report photo. The wooded area itself was just west of and uphill from the gulley where we had previously found the light. When we transposed the three bearing lines onto current aerial imagery, it revealed the coordinates we believed to be the crash site were on private property. The land parcels in the area have backyards that extend approximately fifty feet from the back of the house. The coordinates were actually on a property line between two parcels of land about twenty-five feet above where the open space starts. If this was the location of the crash, all we had to do was search downhill from the location in the open space to find any remaining debris.

Looking at the crash report photo, we were sure that the debris spread out far more than twenty-five feet, and over the years any remaining debris would be carried downhill by erosion. For this search we decided to contact property owners to ask if we could use a backyard to access the open space area, which would cut a mile off the hike in and out. Thankfully the second property owner we contacted let us through their backyard, and searching downhill from our new coordinates revealed several finds that one would expect at the location of an aircraft crash site. We found bits of torn aluminum, a piece with zinc chromate paint on it, and another larger aluminum piece with sheared rivets, that like the light we found a week earlier, was right on the surface. Getting multiple bearings using our treesearching technique had led us right to the site. To confirm this, I scanned areas along the search line but found no bits further up toward the private property or down toward the foreground hill. Sadly, the hillside beneath the location where we found the additional debris was much like the rest of

On April 16, 2022, the City of San Carlos Parks and Recreation Department paid tribute to the seven servicemen who perished on the stormy night of March 14, 1945. A stone-mounted bronze plaque was placed near the entrance to Big Canyon Park, just a few hundred feet below the area where the R4D impacted the coastal foothills. (City of San Carlos)

the open space area, covered in heavy brush and poison oak, ruling out further searches downhill from the crash site location. Still, we found enough to confirm the location and confirm our unorthodox search technique actually worked.

The R4D-5 crash site was only the fourteenth site my son Paxton and I had been to since we first got into aviation archaeology in 2007, and while it was only the third site we found that had been previously undiscovered, we didn't locate it by ourselves. The prior research of other aviation archaeologists ultimately led us to discover the location where seven men lost their lives and sixteen more were injured back on March 14, 1945.

The aviation archaeology/wreckchasing community feels it is important to research, locate, and document crash sites like these to help keep the memory of these fallen service members alive.

Beautiful night study of C-46E N79978 by photographer William T. Larkins, shot at Oakland, California. Note the stepped windscreen, featured only on the seventeen "E" models built in St. Louis, Missouri. When World War II ended, the contract for additional C-46E models was canceled. (William T. Larkins)

Chapter 8

Fist Fight in the Cabin Not a Factor

Tony Moore and Nicholas A. Veronico

Minutes before its right wing clipped a mountain and spun the war surplus, twin-engine, Curtiss Commando airliner into the boulder-strewn hillside, two passengers got into an altercation with names being called and a punch thrown in the main cabin. The parties were separated and Captain Roy G. White got up from the left seat to ensure that the situation was under control.

Captain White was flying Standard Airlines' C-46E N79978 on the last leg of a trip from New York to Long Beach, California, that had originated on the East Coast on July 11, 1949. The flight made stops at Chicago, Illinois; Kansas City, Kansas; Albuquerque, New Mexico; and was en route to Burbank, California, on the morning of July 12. After the stop at Burbank, Captain White would fly the C-46 another thirty miles south to its final destination at Long Beach.

Upon returning to the cockpit, Captain White radioed the Burbank control tower that he'd like the police standing by to arrest one of the passengers. Thirty minutes after returning to the cockpit, Captain White descended into clouds to set-up for landing at Burbank.

At 7:52 a.m., N79978 flew into the northeastern face of 2,320-foot-tall Chatsworth Peak at the 1,890-foot level. The peak is located in the Santa Susana Pass, 30 miles northwest of Los Angeles and one mile north of the Chatsworth Reservoir. On board was a crew of four and forty-four passengers, including two infants. To the amazement of rescuers, thirteen had survived the crash in varying states of medical distress. At the time of impact, pilots of other aircraft reported the marine layer of stratus cloud was 2,400-feet deep, just enough to obscure Chatsworth Peak from the pilot's view. Survivors reported the impact came within two or three minutes of descending into the clouds.

Captain Roy G. White

Co-pilot Harold Tucker

C-46E N79978

The Curtiss C-46E operating that day was different from its sister ships in having a stepped windscreen, which was unique to the E model and different from the streamlined glass cockpit windows of other models. The former freighter had a single cargo door on the port side, and was powered by twin, 2,200 hp Pratt & Whitney R-2800-75 engines driving three-blade propellers. Typically, the C-46s were fitted with R-2800-51 radial engines turning four-blade propellers.

Curtiss built seventeen E models at the company's St. Louis, Missouri-factory as part of a 570 aircraft order, of which 553 were canceled as World War II drew to a close. Serial number 43-47410, manufacturer's serial number 2936, was delivered on July 17, 1945, after the war in Europe had ended, but victory over Japan was still to come. This Commando's assignments kept her within the continental United States until assigned to the War Assets Administration at Clinton, Oklahoma, on February 9, 1947. Fourteen months later, she was sold to Trans National Airlines on April 5, 1948, and registered N79978. This aircraft was operated in the colors of Trans National Airlines' subsidiary Standard Airlines, and flown on non-scheduled passenger flights.

Crash map drawn for the Los Angeles Times *newspaper showing the area of impact, west of Chatsworth. (LA Times Photographic Archives/UCLA Library Special Collections)*

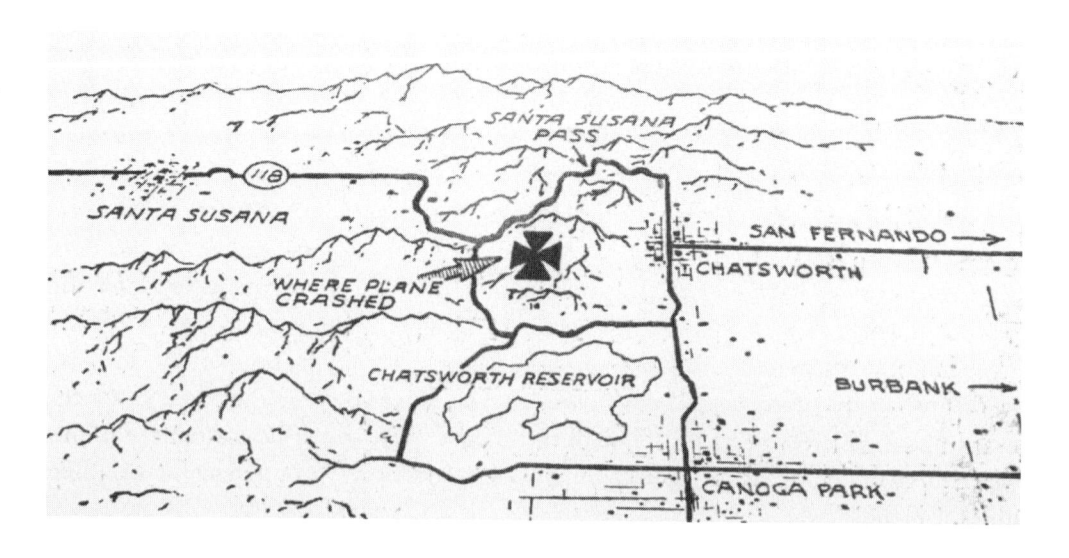

Illustration from the Los Angeles Times *showing the point of impact, the direction the C-46 traveled as its starboard wing ground across the terrain, and the airliner's final resting place. (LA Times Photographic Archives/ UCLA Library Special Collections)*

On the Scene

Descending through thick fog, the Commando initially made contact with some greasewood bushes before the starboard propeller bit into an eight-foot-tall boulder. The C-46 then cartwheeled horizontally across the face of Chatsworth Peak, coming to rest with the fuselage facing uphill. The impact opened up the starboard wing, destroying the structure and splaying its contents – cowling, cowl flaps, propeller blades, flaps, ailerons, and fuel tanks, across a 150-foot-long area, consuming the mountainside's brush in the resulting fire.

The remainder of the aircraft, its fuselage and port wing, came to rest facing up the steep, 60-degree slope and having turned 90-degrees to starboard of the intended flight path. The distance from initial contact to where the fuselage came to rest was only 360 feet.

Much to his own amazement, passenger Robert E. Steinweg was able to get out of the wreckage and, although injured, make his way more than a mile down the fire road to the home of Frank Borden. Here Steinweg was given first aid, and first responders were called. Borden and Mrs. Harley F. Harrison then made their way to the crash scene.

In addition to the smoldering wreckage and walking wounded, Borden and Mrs. Harrison were greeted by Krishna Venta and one of his disciples, Brother Paul. Venta and Brother Paul lived in a stone house monastery in nearby Box Canyon. They heard the early morning impact and explosion. Making their way to the crash site, bare-footed, the pair were able to help the injured, guide the first arriving ambulances, and assist in extricating the dead.

The Santa Susanna and Simi Volunteer Fire Departments were some of the first to the scene of the accident. Ambulances came from the nearby cities of Chatsworth, Fillmore, San Fernando, Simi Valley, and Van Nuys, as well as points farther out in the county including Oxnard, Santa Paula, Ventura, and the Naval Air Missile Test Center at Point Mugu.

Side view of the crash looking east with dozens of first responders making their way to the crash site. Volunteer fire fighters, ambulance crews, and rescue workers from the Pt. Mugu naval air station all gathered to render aid to the survivors. (LA Times Photographic Archives/UCLA Library Special Collections)

First on the scene were Krishna Venta, left with headband, and Brother Paul, right, who helped guide first responders to the crash site and assisted in move the injured down the hill to waiting ambulances. The religious men lived in a monastery in nearby Box Canyon. (LA Times Photographic Archives/UCLA Library Special Collections)

Actress and dancer Caren Marsh survived the crash, albeit severely injured. She was told she'd never dance again due to injuries to her ankle. (LA Times Photographic Archives/UCLA Library Special Collections)

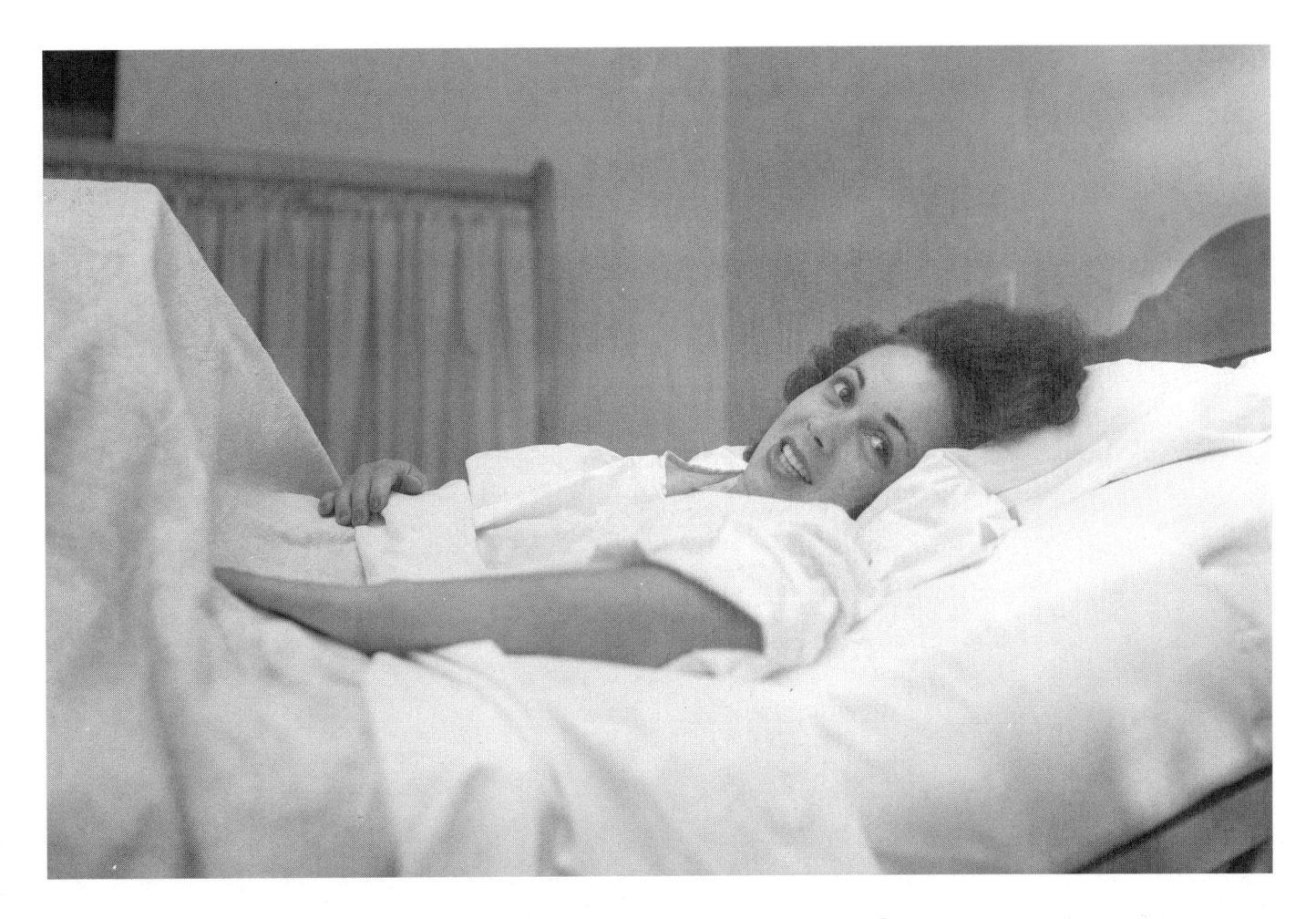

Among the thirteen survivors was thirty-year-old actress and dancer Caren Marsh, who had been Judy Garland's stand-in on the set of *The Wizard of Oz* and had an uncredited part in *Gone with the Wind*. Marsh's ankle was destroyed and doctors felt she would never dance again, but after years of therapy, in the mid-1950s she was able to transition from an acting to a dancing career.

Stewardess Marianne Rose had been ejected from the fuselage during the crash and landed in a hole in the ground. As she flew through the brush, the foliage closed above her, shading her from the rescuers' view. Simi Valley volunteer fireman Harry G. Moody just happened to peer into the hole and spotted Rose. She was extracted from the pit and taken to the hospital. Unfortunately, she succumbed to her injuries a few days later.

Prior to the crash, Standard Airlines' chief stewardess Vicky Zelsdorf had separated the two sparing parties in the cabin. In order to separate the two amateur pugilists, she traded seats with the older of the two gentlemen. The man sitting in Zelsdorf's seat perished in the crash, while the stewardess survived, albeit seriously injured.

Newspaper headlines the following morning exclaimed, "Investigators Doubt Fight in Plane Caused Crash That Cost 35 Lives." Stewardess Charolette Grenander, who survived the crash with a broken leg, cuts and bruises, said the fight between two passengers occurred about 45 minutes before the crash and was settled within fifteen minutes. The man who started the fight was identified as Frank Conway of Albany, N.Y., who perished in the crash. The stewardess was unable to identify the second combatant. She related that the plane's pilot, Captain Roy G. White, had come back to ensure that the fight had been settled.

Detective Sgt. A.M. McDaniel of the Los Angeles County Sheriff's Aero Detail said of the accident in his July 25, 1949, report, "Investigation revealed this plane to have been flying a southwesterly course in level flight with the gear down. The right wing-tip brushed the side of the hill, pulling the plane around 90 degrees. It hit the ground and bounced through the air approximately 300 feet to its final position, headed at a right angle to its original path of flight. In the wreckage was found an altimeter registering 1,940 feet. This altitude was later checked with a calibrated altimeter and found to be correct. This crash location is on course with the normal instrument letdown procedure for Lockheed Airport, but the altitude normally used at this point is 4,000 feet."

Then and now: Aerial of the crash site on the afternoon of the crash. The marine layer has burned off and the skies are sunny. Notice the large number of emergency vehicles including a number of fire trucks and ambulances. The contact scar is visible, seen strewn with C-46 parts. Drone comparison photo shows additional jeep trails that have appeared over the years along with the road cut through the crash site. (LA Times Photographic Archives/UCLA Library Special Collections and Tony Moore)

In the post-crash investigation, the CAB determined that the fight was of no significance in the accident. The plane was too low on approach at that geographic location, and should have been at 5,000 feet. Surviving passenger Mrs. Jewell Frost testified, "We were in a terrible layer of clouds – the fog was so thick we couldn't see the wings. If anything is to blame it was the fog." Airline President Stanley D. Weiss said after the investigation, "I can't grasp what could have caused the accident. There is nothing to show why White was at the altitude (1,940 feet), when he should have been flying at 4,755."

Non-Sked Airline Issues

Standard Airlines was one of the many non-scheduled airlines that popped-up in the post-war years. Known as "non-skeds," these were one of the many post-war opportunities for servicemen to acquire ex-military transport aircraft at a deep discount. The airline was headquartered at Long Beach, California, and was granted its operating certificate, No. 6-14, on February 10, 1947. Standard Airlines was subsequently issued a letter of registration, No. 826, on March 19, 1948. There were four primary transcontinental non-skeds, Standard Airlines being the largest of the group.

Standard Airlines ran afoul of the Civil Aeronautics Board (CAB) in setting up a regular schedule for its cross-country routes as its operating certificate was for "non-scheduled and irregular" flights. At the time, the major, scheduled carriers were closely monitoring the non-skeds, and putting pressure on the CAB to end competition from these low-cost carriers. The major carriers would eventually succeed in ending the era of non-sked operations.

On June 21, 1949, the CAB revoked Standard Airlines' operating permit, but the airline had filed a petition with the U.S. Court of Appeals and was operating while the case moved through the courts. On July 21, nine days after the accident, the U.S. Court of Appeals for the District of Columbia rejected Standard Airlines' petition and ordered the carrier to cease all operations. Although it was out of business, six lawsuits were subsequently filed against the airline and its insurance carrier relating to the crash and loss of life on board N79978.

The Crash Site Today

The final resting place of C-46E N79978 sits in the rugged hills between the San Fernando Valley and Simi Valley where the Simi Hills meet the Santa Susana Mountains. And although Highway 118 passes less than a mile to the north, this is remote country. There are lots of high ridges and deep canyons in the area. During the summer and fall, temperatures will range into the high 80s and low 100s.

The area where N79978 came to rest has changed little in the past 74 years. There are a few more jeep trails that lead to various private properties around the area, but they are not paved and most are gated. A road has been cut through the middle of the crash site putting the area where the C-46 came to rest on the west side with the point of impact and the resulting scar on the east side.

The hillside is strewn with boulders and low-growing buck brush. Glancing up the hillside, the scar where the C-46 careened across the face of the peak is still visible. Nothing has grown where the airliner's fuel saturated the ground and burned the vegetation in the post-crash fire. Little has changed in the rock formations that were present at the time of the crash and photos from the incident are easily lined-up with the terrain.

Close-up of the aircraft's impact trail and the Commando's final resting place. Note the amount of debris in the impact trail as well as the myriad of large boulders on the peak. Drone photo shows the road cut through the crash site and the clearing where the wreckage lay. Due to the amount of aviation fuel deposited on the hillside, nothing has grown where the fuselage came to rest. (LA Times Photographic Archives/ UCLA Library Special Collections and Tony Moore)

The dead are removed from the C-46 wreckage. This crash happened at a different time. There is no caution tape to keep curious people out of the incident scene. In the center of the image, near the fuselage is a photographer with a large format camera on a tripod. While thankful that they were on hand to record the scene, things were certainly different back then. Compare the rock formations between the then and now photos. (LA Times Photographic Archives/UCLA Library Special Collections and Nicholas A. Veronico)

And although the wreckage was removed after the crash investigation, small pieces of the aircraft still litter the site. Lots of internal fittings, hydraulic lines, snaps, and other bits from inside the fuselage structure and wings were located after a short search in the brush below the wreck's final position. The authors then set about matching and recreating the old accident report and newspaper photographs by lining up landmarks noted in the images. Several of those old "then" photographs were aerials, taken by a small aircraft just after the crash, which the authors reshot using a camera drone that retraced the C-46's last fatal seconds.

Investigators comb through the wreckage of N79978 on the side of Chatsworth Peak. Newspapers of the time described the terrain where the C-46E came to rest as having house-sized boulders. Looking down from the crash site one such rock dominates the surrounding brush. (LA Times Photographic Archives/UCLA Library Special Collections and Nicholas A. Veronico)

All that remains at the crash site today are small, internal fittings. (Nicholas A. Veronico)

A road was cut through the crash site which affords a great view into the San Fernando Valley. N79978 was descending into clouds and should have been at 4,000 feet, enabling it to turn to the east over Chatsworth Peak and line up for the runway at Burbank Airport, in the distance to the right. (Nicholas A. Veronico)

David Trojan and Jeff Benya next to plane wreckage that was discovered in a swamp.

Chapter 9
Michigan Crash Site Mystery

David Trojan

The mystery began in 2016 when a gentleman bought a 40-acre parcel of land located about two miles southwest of the old Wurtsmith Air Force Base in Oscoda, Michigan. The previous property owners told him, "A T-33 jet trainer crashed on the property sometime in the 1950s and the two French pilots parachuted to safety." Furthermore, he was told that the Air Force brought in a dozer to push through the swamp to the crash site to be able to take the good parts and then buried the rest of the plane. The property owner Googled T-33 plane crashes in the area, but he could only find two and neither were close to the property. He searched his newly acquired property and found a dozer path through the swamp to a site where he found a piece of aluminum about the size of a crumpled coffee can and some sort of linkage that appeared to have come from a plane. The site is difficult to access because it is located in a dense swamp. The property owner could understand why the Air Force would not try to salvage the whole plane, and he doesn't know how they got to it with 1950s-era equipment.

The new owner was curious about the mysterious crash, so he contacted Jeff Benya of Michigan Aviation Archaeology. Benya and I began a search to identify the site by checking the Aviation Archaeological Investigation and Research website's database for United States military aircraft accident reports. The database includes all Air Force aircraft accidents through 1955, but nothing there seemed to fit the Michigan site. At first glance, the "French" connection did not make much sense. There were French units that trained at Oscoda Air Force Base during World War II, but training of the Free French airmen officially ended in September 1945, and none were in two-seat aircraft. At this point, many questions remained unanswered. If there were indeed French pilots visiting the area after World War II for an airshow or joint training,

Aircraft wreckage discovered by the property owner.

would they have brought their own planes? Did the French Air Force use T-33s? If there was an accident involving French pilots, who would have the accident report? What still remained at the crash site? Could the wreckage at the site help to identify the aircraft?

The first bit of information that we checked was the reference to the T-33 jet fighter. Research revealed that the Lockheed T-33 Shooting Star, two-pilot trainer made its first flight in 1948. The T-33 was used by more than thirty nations including the French Air Force, which had 163 of them. The T-33 Shooting Star was known to have been extensively flown at Oscoda Air Force Base, which changed its name to Wurtsmith in 1953, so the Shooting Star was a definitely a possibility. The database records check did reveal a total of about six possible aircraft accidents between World War II and 1955 that seemed to fit the general location information. There were several possible World War II French P-47s and American F-80, F-86, and T-33 jets that

T-33 Jet Trainer assigned to Oscoda/Wurtsmith AFB Michigan.

crashed in the general area as well. However, the original information was specifically that there was one plane with a crew of two. Upon further examination, none of the possible aircraft accidents in the database matched the description of the crash site or specific location.

The challenge with this investigation was trying to identify which aircraft had crashed at the location. The only way to do that was to investigate the crash site and look for identifying marks such as part numbers and manufacturer inspection stamps. Hopefully the onsite exploration would narrow down the type of plane or manufacturer.

Hints at the Crash Site

An expedition to the crash site was undertaken in September 2016. The site is located in a remote, nasty, overgrown swamp at the bottom of a hill. At first glance nothing is unusual about the site, except the clearing in the heavily wooded area and the pond of water in the middle of it. The pond is surrounded by pieces of metal that are heavily encrusted by vegetation and stuck in the ground. Freeing a piece of metal from the grasp of the swamp required considerable effort. Probing and fishing in the water hole indicated that there were large pieces of metal in it. The largest pieces found were a section of wing and a landing gear door. All the pieces were heavily corroded which made identification very difficult. Only two pieces of wreckage had part numbers and only one had North American Aviation (NAA) manufacturer marks.

We had narrowed down the list of possible aircraft considerably by exploring the crash site and finding NAA markings. North American Aviation made many different aircraft including the T-6 Texan trainer, P-51 Mustang fighter, B-25 Mitchell bomber, and the F-86 Sabre jet fighter. All of these aircraft were based at Oscoda/Wurtsmith AFB at one time or another. However, we could not match any of the part numbers to a specific type of aircraft because we did not have all the parts manuals.

Based on the possible visual match of the landing gear door, the F-86 Sabre jet seemed to fit the original story best. It was still unknown which F-86 model it was or when the crash occurred. The history of Wurtsmith indicates that F-86s were used

Uncovering the aircraft wreckage.

Piece of aircraft with ANA 966 stamp on it which was a manufactures mark for North American Aviation, the other mark is HT for heat treatment of the part.

by the 63rd Fighter Interceptor Squadron (FIS) between January 1951 and August 1955. The 63rd FIS used F-86As in 1951, received F-86Fs in late 1952, F-86Ds in May 1954, and then switched to F-89Ds in the spring of 1955. They operated from O'Hare Airport, Chicago, Illinois, from 1955 to 1958, flying the F-86D/L. It was time to return to the database and search for F-86 Sabre jet accidents. It took months to acquire several complete accident reports for review to see if one matched the Oscoda site. However, once again, none fit the location nor what was discovered in the swamp.

We believed that the wreck was most likely a Wurtsmith-based aircraft, but the other possibility was that it could be a transient aircraft that was visiting the base. The accident could have also occurred after the database's ending date of 1955, or it could be a foreign military aircraft. The only way to eliminate these possibilities was to check the local newspaper archives. Many more months passed by until a researcher was hired to methodically check the local newspaper records. It took more than five hours and fifty dollars for a record check for the time period of 1954 through 1958. Still no matches could be found. We needed the local newspaper checked from 1940-1954 and from 1959 onward.

At this point, the identification of the aircraft still eluded us. We found some wreckage, but which one and what was the story behind it? All we knew was that it was made by North American Aviation. Progress on this investigation stalled as other projects took priority.

Aircraft wreckage dug out of the swamp after considerable effort.

F-86 jet assigned to the 63rd Fighter Interceptor Squadron at Oscoda early 1950s.

Months and then years passed before I decided to renew the search again. I posted all that I knew along with pictures of the wreckage onto the Wreckchasing Message Board website in early 2020. Within days the responses started arriving regarding possible answers to the challenge of the wreckage.

Another researcher determined that the rivet pattern did not match the F-86 gear door and neither did the position of the actuator on the door. It was close, but not quite. The "stars and bars wing panel" had a raised fence that would indicate the airflow direction, making this the outer wing panel fragment of a straight-winged aircraft. The fence and insignia position looked similar to that of a P-51 Mustang, but the oval access panel was in the wrong position for a P-51D model. It was hard to find good pictures of P-51 wings that showed the access cover and the fence in the right position on the aft edge of the outer wing in front of the aileron. Earlier models of the P-51 wings were shaped differently from the later models and the access cover was also different.

Landing gear door emerges from the swampy terrain.

Aircraft Type Identified

The NAA prefix 117-part number found on the one piece of wreckage was also a puzzle because it was not found in any common NAA references and was not used on the P-51D. Furthermore, the part number was too early in the NAA sequence to be from an F-86 Sabre. It was eventually determined that the NAA part number prefix 117 was allocated for a production batch of P-51H aircraft. The other part number that we found was for a carburetor air filter. Research determined that it was used on Cessna-type aircraft among others. What we had found was not a Cessna, but it did eliminate jet-type aircraft because of their lack of carburetors. The aircraft type we found had to be a piston engine aircraft with a carburetor. Lastly, most pictures of the P-51 Mustang show the wheel gear door in the up position. We needed to try to match the landing gear wheel door that we found with P-51H models. We still

Landing gear door from crash site compared to F-86 gear door.

Pilot Captain Harold Howard Buth

were not sure what exactly we had found, but we needed to take a much closer look at P-51 Mustang accidents in the area.

The last confirmation for the identification of the crash site came from P-51 Mustang parts manuals. We were able to match the two parts we found with numbers in the manuals. We were also able to match other parts from the crash site to drawings in the manuals.

The last Michigan unit to fly the P/F-51 Mustang was the 172nd FIS, which flew the type until 1954. Furthermore, many Air National Guard units from other states flying Mustangs visited the Oscoda area gunnery range until it closed around 1959. A bit of digging back into the records found reference to TF-51H serial number 44-64711, which crashed on June 26, 1951. Its crash location was listed as seven miles from Oscoda AFB, and was outside our previous research area. At the time there was no standard way to measure crash locations, but it now made sense that this accident could be the one located in the swamp. A cabin was also referenced in the report that matched one on the forty-acre parcel of land that the new property owner had purchased. The TF-51H was a late model modified version of the P-51 Mustang. The puzzle began to take shape when comparing what we had found and was written in the accident report for 44-64711.

The Final Flight

The official accident report for TF-51H, s/n 44-64711, contained the following edited information. The pilot, Capt. Harold Howard Buth, was flying this aircraft on a proficiency training flight on June 26, 1951. He was very experienced and well qualified to fly this type of aircraft. He had qualified as a pilot on June 5, 1945, and had accumulated 1,554 total flying hours. His primary duty assignment with the squadron was as a flight leader. Capt. Buth and the aircraft were assigned to the 56th Fighter Interceptor Wing, 56th Fighter Interceptor Group, 63rd FIS based at Oscoda. The TF-51H Mustang had accumulated a total of 880 hours flying time. It was reported that the aircraft had experienced engine problems during the weeks leading up to June 26, but had passed preflight checks. It was typical late spring weather for the area with temperature of sixty-one degrees, fifty-percent overcast, ten-mile visibility, and winds from the south-southeast at twelve knots.

Approximately twelve minutes after takeoff, the pilot called the control tower at Oscoda. He reported engine trouble about ten miles from the base and was returning for an emergency landing. At about the same time, an employee of the forestry service stated that he saw the aircraft overhead and noted that its engine sounded as if it was not running well. He saw the aircraft make a turn toward the base and, when last seen, it was losing altitude with its engine cutting in and out.

Approximately two minutes after his original call to the control tower, the pilot called again and said he was lined up with the runway about five miles from the field at 1,500 feet altitude with 140 mph airspeed. The pilot also stated that he was probably going to bail out. This was his last radio transmission. The control tower operator did

Comparison of wing wreckage to P-51 Mustang wing.

not see the aircraft crash. Another F-51 Mustang flying locally was directed to search for the wreckage and, when found, lead rescue crews to the scene. Almost an hour had elapsed from the time of the accident until the first rescue personnel arrived to the crash site.

In Capt. Buth's case, he did what most pilots would do. As soon as he encountered engine problems, he headed back to the base. Unfortunately, he could no longer keep the aircraft in the air and he was too low to bail out. He just ran out of time and altitude. Captain Harold Buth was twenty-nine years old at the time of his death. He left behind a wife and two children, and is buried in the Allouez Catholic Cemetery in Green Bay, Wisconsin.

The crash site is located in a densely wooded, swampy area, less than three miles from the end of the base's longest runway. There were no dwellings other than

Carburetor Air Induction System photos match between manual and wreckage.

a hunting cabin within a mile. There was a definite path of entry through the trees where the aircraft came down. At the point of impact, the aircraft was traveling due east and hit the ground at about a 45-degree angle in a nose down position with wings level. The aircraft's landing gear and flaps were in the up position. The plane came to an immediate stop after chopping the tops off numerous trees and then nosing into the soft ground. The engine and propeller were torn loose and ricocheted off or through more than a dozen trees before coming to a stop about seventy-five feet beyond the fuselage. All engine parts were broken or damaged to such an extent that information could not be obtained from them to determine the cause of the mechanical failure. The fuselage remained fairly intact after impact; however, the fuselage center section was completely burned. The pilot's body was found about eighty feet before the point of impact. Investigators concluded that he did not have enough time or altitude to open his parachute or that he hit the tail of the aircraft on his way out. With the permission of the land owner, the wreckage was buried in the swamp after it was determined that it was virtually impossible to reclaim anything for salvage or further investigation.

P-51H Operations

The P-51H was the ultimate version of the Mustang, which was the fastest Mustang variant to enter production during World War II. However, it did not see combat because it entered service too late. The P-51H had redesigned wings and undercarriage, lengthened fuselage, taller tail, and was almost 600 pounds lighter compared to the earlier P-51D model. That is why I was unable to match the wreckage earlier to a P-51D model. The P-51H was powered by the uprated Packard Merlin V-1659-9 engine that gave it a top speed of 487 mph, which was more than fifty mph faster than the P-51D.

In 1947, the designation system changed from pursuit to fighter and the P-51H was re-designated as F-51H. On September 1, 1947, the F-51H participated in the United States Army Air Forces flight (USAAF) demonstration at the National Air Races in Cleveland, Ohio. The "T" designation was added some time later and was used to indicate that the aircraft was relegated to training duties. The TF-51H may

P-51H s/n 44-64319 of the 56th Fighter Group. (USAF Photo)

P-51H serial number 44-64675.

have been used as a target for radar intercept training. According to a source in Oscoda, the "T" designation indicated that it was used as a tug for towing gunnery target sleeves.

TF-51H, s/n 44-64711, was one of the last Mustangs built by North American Aviation at its Inglewood, California, factory. Originally manufactured as a P-51H-10-NA, it was delivered on November 30, 1945. In total, NAA produced 555 P-51H Mustangs (44-64160 to 44-64714) under USAAF contract number AC 1752. These included twenty P-51H-1-NA, 280 P-51H-5-NA, and 255 P-51H-10-NA. In early 1946, the P-51H was assigned to the Strategic Air Command, Fifteenth Air Force, 56th Fighter Interceptor Group (FIG) at Selfridge Field, Michigan. The 56th FIG was assigned as a long-range fighter escort unit for B-29 Superfortress bombers.

My research analysis for the time period revealed some staggering statics: During the twenty-four-month period from January 1, 1950, to January 1, 1952, there were 462 major accidents involving F-51 Mustangs. Pilots were found responsible for approximately 40 percent of the accidents and the other 60 percent were material failures. The accident rate per 100,000 flight hours jumped from ninety-three in 1949, to 109 in 1950, to 279 in 1951. Clearly the numbers of accidents dramatically increased during that time and most were due to equipment failures. During the early 1950s, jet-powered fighters became the new standard, forcing the retirement and wholesale replacement of propeller driven fighters. The last F-51H Mustangs were retired from Air National Guard units in 1957.

Reflections on the Mystery Crash Site

In conclusion, this crash site investigation took several years to solve, but lessons were learned. The investigation required onsite exploration as well as years of database records examination, but was concluded with help from the internet Wreckchasing Message Board. There was very little truth in the original story and only the fact that a plane did crash during the 1950s was accurate. The part about the French connection and T-33 jet were incorrect. There are many legends about French fliers training in northern Michigan and most likely the stories got mixed up. The original, incorrect information about a T-33 jet type aircraft persuaded me to initially believe that what we had found was a jet-type aircraft. I was proved wrong. The lesson learned is that it is best to seek out the opinions and knowledge of others. They just may be able to save you time and help solve the mystery.

Beechcraft built 1,582 examples of the AT-11 during World War II as a bomber/gunnery trainer. The aircraft's bomb bay could hold ten 100-pound practice bombs and was equipped with a Crocker-Wheeler top turret. The aircraft's designation was changed to T-11 in 1948. (USAAF photo)

Chapter 10

Searching for Answers at a Beech T-11 Wreck Site

David Trojan

On April 12, 1953, during a flight to Portland, Oregon, a Beech T-11 Kansan trainer, United States Air Force serial number 42-37572, went missing. This story is about the aircraft accident and one man's search for answers about why it crashed. After an expedition to the crash site, aviation archaeologists were finally able to clarify the details of the accident.

The pilot of the missing T-11 was Capt. Robert Vernon Blucher, who was recalled to active duty on February 7, 1953. He was assigned to the 4704 Defense Wing, 567th Operations Squadron as assistant base operations officer at McChord Air Force Base, Washington. Blucher was from Caldwell, Idaho. He was an eager pilot who wanted to fly and appeared confident in all his flights. He was checked out in the Beech T-11 Kansan, de Havilland L-20 Beaver, and Douglas C-47 Skytrain, having logged over seventy hours within a two-month period while assigned to McChord. His total flying hours was far above the time an average pilot assigned to the base would have acquired. According to the operations officer, Blucher had devoted much more time toward flying and not enough attention to his other duties. Blucher had a total of more than 1,800 flying hours and over 560 hours in the T-11 aircraft.

The Beech T-11 Kansan bombardier/gunnery trainer aircraft was a military version of the twin-engine Beechcraft Model 18 commercial transport. Modifications included a transparent nose, a bomb bay and internal bomb racks, and a top gun turret. The T-11 Kansan was used to train more than 90 percent of all American bombardiers during and after World War II. The T-11 could carry ten 100-pound general purpose or practice bombs. Beech built 1,582 T-11 trainers and serial number 42-37572 was manufactured October 26, 1943. In June 1948, the trainer was re-designated as a T-11. The accident aircraft, 42-37572, had logged more than 3,700 hours since it was manufactured.

Inside a T-11 Kansan loaded with bombs. (USAF photo)

Crash site located in thick forest. Photo from accident report.

USAF T-11 Goes Missing

Capt. Blucher departed McChord on April 12 at the controls of 42-37572, en route to Portland, a distance of 130 miles. Weather at the time was reported as 3,000 scattered and fifteen miles visibility, but the weather deteriorated rapidly as the flight progressed. Blucher landed safely in Portland and refueled, then departed at 10:20 a.m. local time for Eugene. He arrived at 11:03. He departed Eugene at 12:47 p.m., en route to Redmond, Oregon, where he arrived at 2:20 p.m. At 6:53 p.m., Blucher took off from Redmond for Portland via The Dalles, the largest city of Wasco County, Oregon. He was last reported over The Dalles at 8:25 p.m., at an altitude of 4,000 feet. His estimated time of arrival at Portland was planned for 10:56 p.m., but he never arrived. He was declared missing the following morning.

An intensive search for Blucher's Beech T-11 was started the next morning by the Air Force and Civil Air Patrol. According to news reports, the pilot was last sighted over Hood River en route to Portland. He radioed The Dalles that he was running short of gas and was returning to the airport there. No further radio contact was reported. More than twenty civilian and military planes joined in the search over Skamania County, Washington, and the Cascade Locks, Oregon, area to look for signs of wreckage. At first, the searchers hoped to find the missing plane on a river bar. As the search continued, observers examined the surrounding hills and several miles inland. Heavy timber forest covered most of the area, and aircraft searched the same areas as many as five times to adequately cover the rough terrain. A total of 202 sorties spanning 438 hours were flown looking for the missing aircraft. Searchers were generally of the opinion that the plane must have struck a hillside in poor weather. The intensive search was abandoned April 23, 1953, after no trace of the aircraft was found.

Six months later, on October 24, 1953, a deer hunter happened upon the wrecked plane in the middle of the forest. The badly broken and scattered wreck was located in the deep woods between mountains at approximately the 3,300-foot level. Examination of the wreckage revealed that the airplane had been climbing at the time of the crash and was flying in a southerly direction attempting to cross the ridge. Mountain peaks in the area averaged 3,500 feet. Trees in the vicinity were 150-200 feet high and the forward part of the fuselage was found hanging in the trees twenty to twenty-five feet off the ground. The aircraft did not burn upon contact with the trees, but the airframe was ripped apart. There was evidence of small gasoline fires that were evidently put out by the rain on the night of the accident. Dental records and personal effects were used to positively identify the pilot's remains. Capt. Robert Vernon Blucher was thirty-one years old at the time of his death. He is buried at the Greenwood Cemetery, Bend, Oregon.

Exactly what happened during the flight will never be known. The Accident Investigation Board concluded that Blucher flew into deteriorating weather conditions while on a Visual Flight Rules (VFR) clearance. It was further believed that he attempted to circumnavigate the weather and got off course to the north in an attempt to get back to the Columbia River Valley. Blucher crashed when he was unable to clear a mountain ridge. Despite the experience and skill of the pilot, the weather got the best of him. The Air Force felt that the inaccessibility of the aircraft wreckage precluded economical reclamation, so the aircraft wreck was left in place, written off, and almost forgotten.

Vertical stab Wreckage of T-11, 42-37572 in the trees. Photos from the accident report.

The group carefully examined the wreckage. Aviation Archaeologists were able to identify all the major parts and several details that Armen Woosley had missed during his previous trips to the wreck. (Dave McCurry)

The weather cooperated and it was a beautiful day to go hiking. The wreck is located in a saddle at approximately the 3300-foot level between mountains near Grassy Knoll northwest of Willard, Washington. (David Trojan)

The largest piece of wreckage is inspected. This appears to be the underside of the fuselage with the bomb bay showing. (Armen Woosley)

The letter "U" from USAF on the wing. (Armen Woosley)

Large empennage section upside down against a tree. (Sam Parker)

One engine was missing several cylinder heads that had been unbolted and removed. Who salvaged the wreck and when is unknown. (Sam Parker)

Weather-beaten star and bar insignia on a piece of wing. (Armen Woosley)

Numerous bomb racks and shackles were at the site. They confirmed that the Beech T-11 was in the bombardier training configuration. (David Trojan)

In Pursuit of the Wreck Site

The T-11 aircraft wreck was nearly forgotten until Armen Woosley became interested in it. Woosley was born in January 1952, and early in his life, maybe as young as three years old, he remembers visiting the Sid Ostroski family. Ostroski had found the military plane wreck on Grassy Knoll northwest of Willard, Washington, while hunting. Ostroski had recovered a few artifacts from the wreck and he showed them to young Woosley. The artifacts included cockpit gauges and an orange-and-white parachute. Woosley thought the artifacts were really neat and they left an impression on the boy. He still remembered seeing the parts more than sixty-four years later.

In 1974, Woosley and his friend Jeff Walker decided to go see the wreck and asked Ostroski for directions. They drove as close as possible to the location and hiked to it with no problems. The aircraft wreckage remained unchanged since it had crashed. Woosley recalled that the plane was torn to pieces and scattered over an acre deep in the forest. He saw parts of the instrument panel, a large piece of fuselage with the star and bar insignia, and a radial engine. Unfortunately, they did not take any pictures at that time. They also did not know the details about the accident and Woosley had lingering questions about the plane and pilot.

Another forty-four years passed before Woosley had his interest rekindled about the wreck. Woosley had become a professional logger and worked in the deep forest for many years. He never forgot about the wreck and he wanted to finally answer questions that he long held. In early 2018, he started gathering information and contacting people

Plugs and wiring were all there, but the radio equipment was missing. It looked like all the equipment had been unplugged and salvaged. (David Trojan)

Remnants of fabric remained on one of the wing flaps dated August 1952. They must have stenciled a date on it after it was changed. (David Trojan)

that might know more. By then he only had a foggy idea where it was located, but he was determined to revisit the crash site and this time learn the story behind the wreck.

Woosley contacted his friend and aviation archeologist David McCurry from Pasco, Washington. A search was planned for early spring, but had to be postponed. On May 21, 2018, Woosley and his friends Lyle Schwarz and fellow logger Greg Koch, again drove as close as possible to the location and hiked into the forest. Schwarz was the first to find a piece of aluminum with rivets in it, so they knew they were close. Within forty-five minutes they located the central mass of the wreckage. By this time someone had salvaged parts of the plane, but most was still there. They photographed the wreck before departing and scouted a better trail back to the crash site.

In June 2018, Woosley did further research in the *Skamania County Pioneer* newspaper for information about the wreck. He discovered articles dating from when the plane was missing and then found in 1953. He learned that his friend Sid Ostroski was not the first one to find the plane as Woosley had been told. Instead, it was a man named Louis Larson, another person Woosley had known when he was a young man. He also found stories about how the Grassy Knoll Lookout was rebuilt during the summer of 1953 by the U.S. Forest Service. They had planes from the military dropping supplies into the crews working on the lookout during the summer of 1953. The crash site is roughly one mile from the lookout, so planes flying in supplies would have flown over the crash site repeatedly throughout that summer and never noticed the wreck.

This large piece is the floor of the aircraft. Both sides and the top of the fuselage were ripped off. A 35mm motion picture camera was mounted in the round hole to film each bomb run to record students bombing scores. (Sam Parker)

Woosley kept in contact with David McCurry hoping to learn more about the wreck and to obtain a copy of the official accident report. On the morning of July 21, 2018, a group led by Woosley began the hike to the T-11 wreck. To reach the location of the crash site required hiking up 900 feet of a 3,500-foot mountain, then descending down several hundred feet into a saddle between mountains.

Through these many years Woosley wanted to know the details of the accident and also the human-interest side of the story. The Air Force accident report and this story have immensely helped tie the details together. Also, having experienced aviation researchers clarify details at the crash site during three visits helped bring closure to his quest for answers.

Today Woosley is working with the son of Sid Ostroski to locate the box of gauges and other artifacts from the wreck that were stored after his dad passed away. Woosley would like to persuade Ostroski to donate the parts to the Skamania County Museum along with this story and accident report to fully convey the local historical event.

Aluminum high up in the tree zoomed in and circled. (Armen Woosley)

The group was able to prop up the left side of the fuselage. In the photo are Vicki McCurry, Lyle Schwarz, David Trojan, Don Hinton, Dave McCurry and Sam Parker.

F-86 similar to the F-86E that was part of a five-ship flight air combat maneuvering training flight from the 3595th Flying Training Group on April 9, 1953. (William T. Larkins)

Chapter 11

Air Combat Maneuvering Results in Stall Spin Accident

James Douglas Scroggins III

What began as a routine training mission, turned out to be a long day for the pilot of an F-86E Sabre jet fighter. On the morning of April, 9, 1953, Lt. Donald Denison was assigned North American F-86E, serial number 51-12983, and was briefed on all facets of the upcoming flight. With 350 hours of total flying time and just thirty-two hours in the F-86, this student pilot was in for the flight of his life!

Taking off from Nellis Air Force Base outside of Las Vegas, Nevada, five F-86s from the 3595th Flying Training Group headed for one of the ranges southeast of the base. The mission profile for the flight was to practice air combat maneuvering by engaging in a mock dogfight. The training mission was led by flight instructor Capt. Howard C. Irish. His wingman was 2Lt. David Mac Kenzie, while pilots of the third and fourth aircraft were not named in the accident report, and the fifth F-86 was flown by Lt. Denison.

About an hour into the exercise, with everything routine to this point, all aircraft formed on Capt. Irish for another in a series of attack maneuvers. This engagement was to be a two-on-two attack with the instructor observing from outside the tactical airspace. A thousand feet in altitude separated the two flights.

Capt. Irish was at approximately 35,000 feet when the two flights intercepted each other, making several turns. The number four and five aircraft were positioned at the higher altitude. Unaware that the aircraft they spotted on this pass was their flight instructor, they began an attack, initiated by number four with Lt. Denison following in the number five jet. The two pilots quickly realized the aircraft they were intercepting was

Doug Scroggins looks over the remains of the right outer wing section.

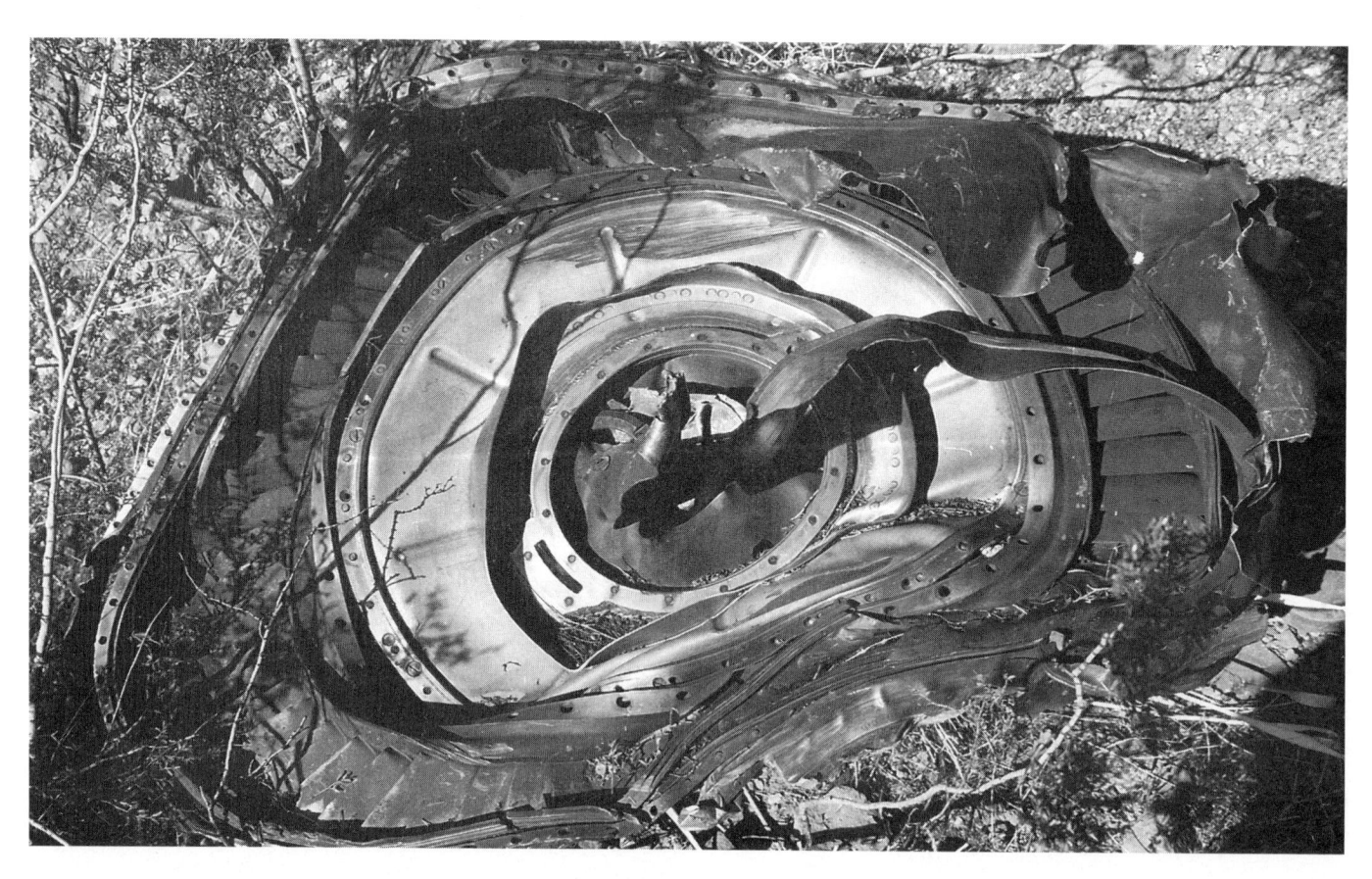

Part of the F-86E's J47-GE-13 engine shows the force of the aircraft's impact with the desert.

Engine rpm indicator found at the crash site.

The Bomb-Target Wind Control and the tachometer were both located in the crash debris.

their flight instructor and broke off. The number four jet broke left while Lt. Denison passed his instructor and began a barrel roll to the left, to keep the aircraft in sight. Meanwhile, the number two and three aircraft witnessed the event from their position.

After completing the barrel roll, Denison's aircraft violently snap-rolled and spun left. The standard recovery from a spin of this type is to push the stick forward and add rudder opposite to the direction of the spin. Despite these efforts, there was no response from the aircraft. The F-86 was now in a vertical spin and Denison's continued efforts proved futile. Checking the altimeter, he thought he saw the needle pass through the 10,000-foot mark and, in a panic, he elected to bail out.

Not knowing which member of his team was in trouble, Capt. Irish made his first radio instructions to the jet, "F-86 in a spin, start your recovery." When it became apparent that the pilot could not affect a recovery, Capt. Irish made his second call, "Bail out...bail out!" Shortly thereafter, the leader watched the aircraft hit the ground and explode.

The moment the Sabre jet hit the ground, Capt. Irish heard "'Chute sighted!" over the radio. As he looked up, Irish spotted a parachute. Climbing up to the suspended aviator's altitude, Irish called for a flight ID check. Numbers two, three, and four checked in, confirming that it was Denison who had hit the silk.

Denison's inexperience in this aircraft and his misreading of the altimeter led to the premature ejection. He survived the incident with minor injuries. Ultimately, the young pilot had several thousand additional feet of altitude with which to affect a recovery from the spin. The accident led to stricter training on the F-86, especially in recovery spin mode. Nellis pilots were not put into mock battle until completely checked out on the aircraft, particularly in aerobatics and high-speed maneuvers in combat. Emphasis was also placed on spin recovery techniques, stall characteristics, and correct interpretation of instruments.

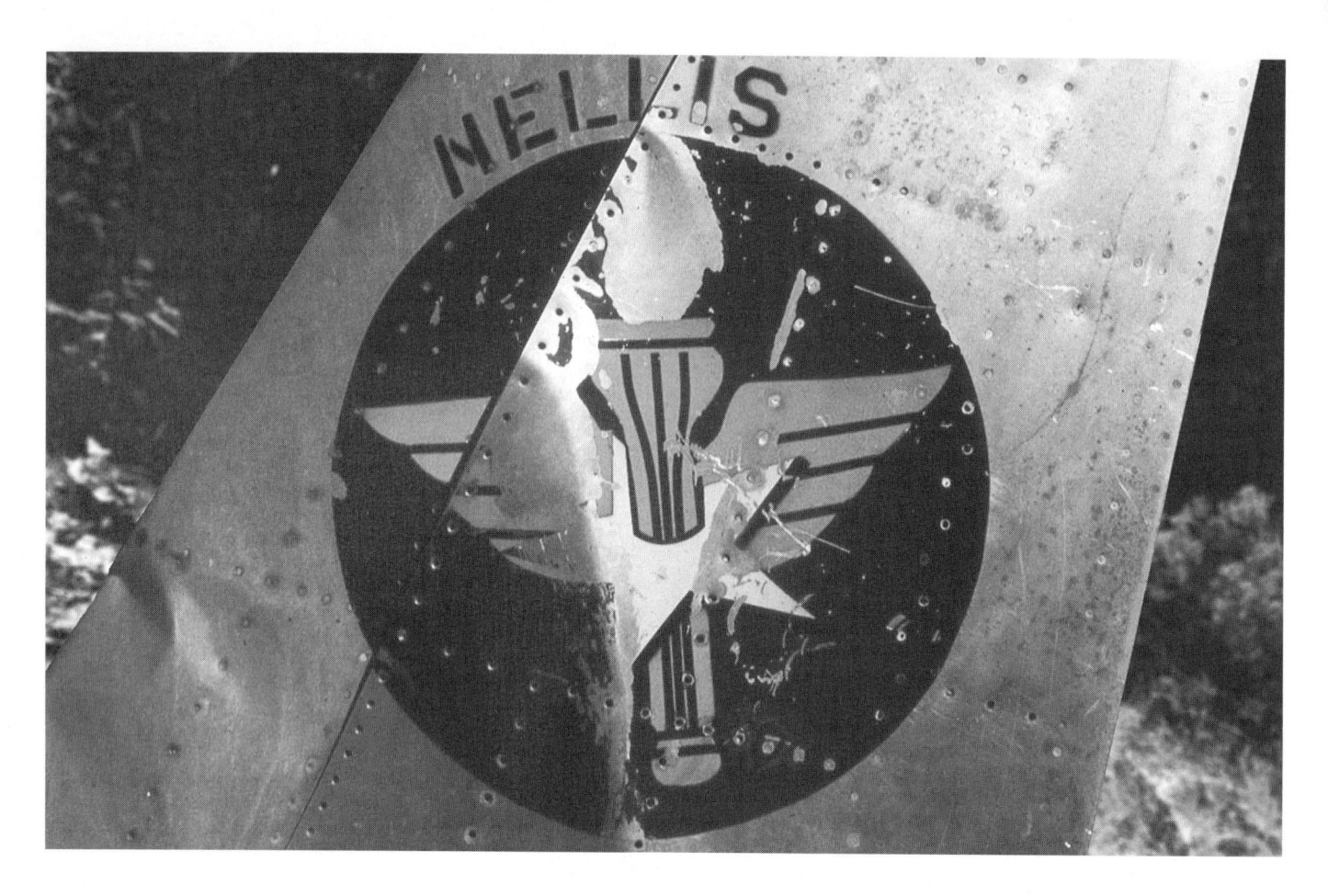

The Nellis Training logo is seen on the port side of the vertical. Albeit worn, the paint was in excellent condition.

F-86 Crash Site Today

Locating the wreckage of the F-86E began one hot summer in Las Vegas. Along with Craig Fuller and Robb Hill, I set out to locate the downed Sabre jet. An arc was plotted around the aircraft's estimated crash location in rugged terrain near Lake Mead, Nevada. Using a Quad-map and a GPS we hiked through the hilly landscape with ground temperatures ranging from 100 to 125 degrees. The high temperatures made the search effort extremely difficult.

Coming up empty-handed, we decided to increase the search area by spreading out over the hills. Within thirty minutes, we set out at a faster pace and moved to higher ground, figuring the higher route would lead to a better vantage point along the top of a mesa.

Suddenly, there it was...something shiny, in a small canyon underneath a steep cliff. At first, I thought I was mistaken, that it was just the sun reflecting off the rocks. Then I spotted what resembled the tail section of the F-86 fighter. I quickly alerted Fuller and Hill to my findings. I proceeded down the hill to find what appeared to be well-preserved wreckage.

We spent two hours at the scene, documenting interesting items, both large and small. Several instruments were discovered, including a tachometer and what is known as a bomb-target wind control unit. The most interesting piece of wreckage was the vertical tail fin with the clear Nellis Air Force Base training logo stenciled on it. The condition of the wreckage indicated that the aircraft impacted at a very low speed, in spite of the fact that it was unmanned. Of all the military jet crashes we felt this is very uncommon for a jet crash. Typically, they are high speed impacts leaving very little behind to identify.

Doug Scroggins displays the tail section of F-86E 51-12983 at the 50th Anniversary of the US Air Force at Nellis AFB in April 1997.

F-100C similar to the aircraft flown by 1Lt. Samuel K. Bacon, Jr. on July 25, 1957, climbs for altitude. Lt. Bacon went missing during a cross-country training flight. (USAF)

Chapter 12

The Legend of Airplane Canyon

David Trojan

There are many stories that are passed down through generations in the western United States to become folklore. This is one such story that was investigated to learn the tragic truth about what happened when an F-100 Super Sabre jet fighter was lost in 1957. This account reveals the truth about what happened to the jet and what remains a legend in the Old West. The setting is Cherry Creek, slowly becoming a ghost town in northcentral Nevada. The main occupations there are hunting, gold prospecting, drinking, and storytelling.

More than 130 years ago the town of Cherry Creek had more than 6,000 residents and twenty-eight saloons. Cherry Creek's largest years of gold and silver production were between 1872 and 1883. One local mine produced more than one million dollars in gold bullion. Just to the south in Egan Canyon, Pony Express riders and stage coaches traveled through the area. Cherry Creek remained the home of several hundred people and the base of substantial mining activity until the 1940s. The town has been fading away since. The post office closed in 1974 and the last saloon closed in 2010. The 2010 census listed seventy-nine residents and currently about twenty people live there in peace and quiet.

Cherry Creek has no businesses, no cell service, and the nearest store and gas station is over fifty miles away in Ely, Nevada. Life there runs at a different pace. It is a place where time is almost forgotten. The town has been described as historic, remote, rural, and uncivilized. In the town a few newer homes are interspersed with the ruins of abandoned buildings. A museum is located in an early one-room schoolhouse that is the second oldest school in Nevada.

1Lt. Samuel Kenneth Bacon Jr. (Courtesy Bacon Family)

Present day Cherry Creek, Nevada. (David Trojan)

Exploring the area is taking a step back in time. There is a sense of history about the place. Walking around town one could easily image horses and miners crowding the streets and almost sense the people who lived out their lives there. Cherry Creek is one of the best places to experience the Old West and is one of the best ghost towns in Nevada. Just don't call it a "ghost town" to any of its few residents! Cherry Creek offers a rare opportunity to see a relatively intact, old-time mining community as well as a relatively intact jet fighter wreck.

The F-100 crash site as viewed across Airplane Canyon. (Craig Fuller)

Missing for twenty-eight days, Lt. Bacon's Super Sabre was finally located on the western slopes of the Egan Mountain Range, northwest of Ely, Nevada. The fighter seems to have mushed into the ground, nearly clearing the ridge. (Craig Fuller)

The paint on the national insignia has had minimal exposure to the elements. (David Trojan)

A Mystery Grows

For many years ranchers, hunters, and miners traveling through a remote, narrow canyon ten miles west of town couldn't help but notice the sun's reflection off something large, shimmering high-up on a mountain side. However, no one was brave or foolhardy enough to venture into the rugged mountains to investigate. Curious rumors began to circulate in town. Could it have come from Area 51, which is not too far away? Soon a legend was born about the mysterious object on the mountain.

The object had been there for as long as anyone could remember. Eventually, curiosity got the best of some locals and the sheriff was called in to investigate.

Relatively intact J57 engine. (David Trojan)

USAF is still readable on the upper surface of the wing. (David Trojan)

He reported back that the reflections were caused by the wreck of an unmanned drone aircraft. He went on to say that it was nothing to worry about and there was nothing to see at the site. However, in this town the citizens are suspicious of the authorities and some locals decided to make the challenging hike up to the site. Besides investigating the site, they could hunt and gold prospect along the way.

A few residents made the long journey along the mining roads and the arduous trek up the steep mountain to the site. Once they arrived, not being knowledgeable about aircraft and because of its condition, the wreck was misidentified as an F-104 jet fighter. The adventurous hikers did take some photos and brought back more stories to share, but found no gold on the mountain. Years passed and more than a few stories were told about how the jet plane got there and its base of origin. The story of the plane wreck was a favorite at the local watering hole before it closed. The remote mountain canyon became known by the locals as "Airplane Canyon."

Torch marks on the wing show where scrappers attempted to harvest aluminum from the wreck site. (David Trojan)

Phase One: Getting to the Site

Eventually the story of the plane wreck on the mountain near Cherry Creek, Nevada, reached this author. Fortunately, one of the last twenty people remaining in the town is the brother of Jerry Bowen, a Vacaville, California, historian. Warren Bowen owns a house in Cherry Creek and is one of the few residents who has studied and collected the town's history. He put me in contact with the residents who had hiked to the site and taken the pictures. Examining the photos, I also could not positively identify the wreck due to its condition. I could see that there was a lot of aircraft wreckage there, but what type was it and why was it there? The investigative hunt began!

Much planning was required to make the long journey to such a remote location. The town is situated above 6,000 feet in high desert country. The crash site is located another 2,000 feet further up into the mountains. A team of professionals was assembled that included an ex-military Joint POW/MIA

Ore car rail container used to melt aluminum under the wing. (David Trojan)

Accounting Command member, a Boeing Co. engineer, a distinguished author and his wife, and myself who is an aviation archaeologist and historian. On a hot June day with the temperatures pushing above 95 degrees and the high altitude taking its toll, we made the long journey to the crash site. Usually, the challenge is finding the crash site, but in this case, we knew the location. We could see the wreck high up on the mountain side near a cliff. The problem was how to get there. The trip required a tough new 4x4 truck to transport us up as high as we could drive. We then had to claw our way up the rough abandoned mining roads to about 7,500 feet. After that there was still another 500 feet of elevation to climb through the dense brush to reach our destination.

While hiking through the wilderness one could hear the birds squabbling and the wind howling. I could image what it was like for gold prospectors seeking treasure as I was experiencing the effort it took to get myself and equipment up the mountain through the rough terrain. I was doing the same thing as the prospectors, but the treasure that I was seeking was the truth about what happened so long ago. I kept wondering what I would discover.

We passed a test mine honed out of the rock by prospectors in search of gold. It was very hard labor to carve out a hole in the rock, only for it to come up empty of gold. The hike was difficult due to the altitude, but the search continued through the thick brush and steep terrain. Several hundred feet from the wreck site we found the first piece of aircraft debris. It was most likely placed there as a guide marker to the site. We knew we were getting close, but we still could not see the aircraft because thick brush obscured our view.

Finally, we broke out into a clearing and the once powerful jet fighter revealed itself along the mountain ridge. It was amazing to see such a sight, the view was spectacular! There before us lay the entire remains of the wrecked plane. We knew instantly that all the effort to reach the crash site was worth it.

Excitement ran high as we each explored the wreck in our own way. I took a moment to take it all in before I started my detailed examination of the parts. Part numbers and data plates confirmed the wreck was a North American F-100C Super

Burned binder rings found at the crash site. (David Trojan)

Sabre. The F-100 Super Sabre was the first United States Air Force operational aircraft to exceed the speed of sound in level flight. The F-100 was not an easy aircraft to fly and one-quarter of all F-100s were lost in accidents.

Phase Two: Assembling the Facts

After arriving home, further research revealed that the F-100 crashed on July 25, 1957, under mysterious circumstances. The pilot, 1Lt. Samuel "Ken" Bacon, was twenty-eight years old at the time. He was a graduate of Brigham Young University and was married with a six-month-old daughter. He also had a brother and two sisters.

History of the flight from the official accident report:

A flight of six F-100 Super Sabre jet aircraft took off on a routine training mission from George AFB at approximately 1300 hours for Webb AFB, Texas, and return to George AFB on 25 July 1957. Pilot 1st Lieutenant Samuel Bacon, was flying in F-100C, serial number 54-2090. Near El Paso Texas it was noticed that Lt. Bacon had taken a position high and in trail of his wingman. Lt. Bacon was then heard to say something to the effect that he was "getting out". When queried by other flight members, he negated his previous statement, saying he was alright and in the clear at 7,000 feet. He then called and said he thought his aircraft was on fire, then denied that and declared that his Heat and Vent Overheat warning light as on and there were fumes in the cockpit. Lt. Bacon was then directed to select the RAM OFF- PRESSURE OFF position on his cockpit pressurization selector and asked, "How do your gauges read?" Lt. Bacon stated that the warning light had gone out and the gauges "read O.K." Lt. Bacon was advised to set a course to the Wink TX radio waypoint and climb to 3,000 feet to rendezvous at Wink TX. The flight, minus Lt. Bacon, proceeded to Wink TX waypoint. Lt. Bacon then apparently flew by mistake to Carlsbad, NM (about 75 miles from Wink TX). The flight was then instructed to select UHF channel #10 for Ground-Controlled Interception (GCI). The GCI site established radar contact with all the aircraft and vectored Lt. Bacon and the others to a rendezvous at Wink. The flight then proceeded to Webb AFB under VFR conditions and GCI control where they all landed.

After landing at Webb AFB, the flight leader received a message advising them to return to George AFB as soon as possible. During the layover Lt. Bacon held a lengthy telephone conversation with a friend and was visited at the flight line by two other friends and their wives, identities unknown. Also during the turn-around time at Webb AFB, the flight leader talked with Lt. Bacon about his losing the flight previously. Lt. Bacon said he had simply lost sight of the leader, when he looked at his instruments, his attitude Gyro was indicating a 45 degree climbing turn to the right, and he thought his instruments were inoperative. During his attempts to right the aircraft, he said, the airspeed dropped to 110 knots then built up to Mach 1, just prior to pull-out. The flight leader asked him if he had been in a spin, to which Lt. Bacon replied he wasn't sure what maneuver he had done.

Some of the flight members noted that Lt. Bacon appeared not to be too well. He assured them he was alright and felt well enough to fly. He had gone to the Flight Surgeon at 0730 hours that morning, complaining of a sore throat and a low down cough. The doctor gave Lt. Bacon APC's (APC - Aspirin, phenacetin, and caffeine) and he was told to gargle and get some rest. The doctor cautioned him against prolonged breathing of 100 % oxygen, as this may cause symptoms of "the chokes" because of the dryness. Formal grounding was never considered.

After determining that each aircraft had sufficient oxygen (all had more than three liters), the flight leader briefed all the pilots for the return flight to George AFB. Flight positions were the same as on the previous leg. The briefing included basic instrument flying, night flying, night formation, vertigo, hypoxia (deficiency in the amount of oxygen), lost flight procedure, lost wingman procedure, loss of radio, loss of flight instruments, emergency airfields en route, weather en route, emergency GCI procedures and the flight profile. Lt. Bacon was further briefed on the relative position he should maintain during the return flight. The flight was to consist of two elements of three aircraft each, with a separation of approximately one minute between elements. All flight members had in their possession flight logs and maps covering the route, which was the reciprocal of the previous route. The entire return flight was to be at one thousand feet "on top". The weather en-route included scattered thunderstorms with heavy turbulence and hail. It was also reported that the maximum cloud tops were at 49,000 feet with heavy icing at 14,000 to 25,000 feet in the thunderstorms.

The flight took off at 2041 (8:41 pm) and climbed to 35,000 feet, then to 42,000 feet, then to 43,000 feet in order to remain 1,000 feet "on top". While approaching El Paso TX, Lt. Bacon's wingmen maintained "fairly close formation" for approximately five minutes, but then Lt. Bacon entered a steep bank toward the element leader and crossed under his aircraft. At about this time he called that he was crossing and re-crossed to his original position. The wingman could "Think of no apparent reason for this maneuver." Subsequently, Lt. Bacon's formation position varied excessively.

As the cloud tops were becoming lower, the flight leader called his element to "close in," so as to descend to a lower altitude. He then repeated the order without response from Lt. Bacon. Immediately there-after Lt. Bacon's aircraft was observed dropping slowly out of sight and into the cloud tops and Lt. Bacon was heard to say that he had lost sight of the flight. Lt. Bacon was then told the heading, altitude and airspeed of the element while the flight began a slow descent to 40,000 feet, remaining 1,000 feet "on top".
Lt. Bacon acknowledged the instructions to maintain his heading and to descent to 40,000 feet. As the cloud tops continued to lower, the flight descended to 38,000 feet, also acknowledged by Lt. Bacon. Approximately five minutes east of Tucson AZ, two aircraft engaged afterburners to assist Lt. Bacon in establishing visual contact, but without success. The heading, altitude and airspeed information was again transmitted and Lt. Bacon was advised to notify the flight when he had a compass swing on Tucson Radio.

Lieutenant Bacon acknowledged the radio call. At 2043 hours Lt. Bacon called that he had a compass swing on Tucson. Lt. Bacon was then instructed to turn to a heading of 284 degrees for Gila Bend AZ Radio, and Lt. Bacon acknowledged. That was the last transmission heard from Lt. Bacon.

A radar search was immediately conducted seventy miles in front of and behind the flight of jets using both height and search radar, but contact could not be established with Lt. Bacon's aircraft. There being nothing further the flight could do, they proceeded to George AFB and landed at approximately 2135 hours. First Lieutenant Samuel K. Bacon Jr. was missing.

Approximately 200 planes were involved in the daily search for the lost jet for almost a month. During the search, telegrams, telephone calls, and thousands of letters were received by the Bacon family from all parts of the world. They expressed the theme: "We are praying for Lt. Bacon's safety." There was a front-page article in the *Los Angeles Times* about how the family offered a $2,500 reward for information about the lost pilot.

The jet crash site was finally located on August 20, after twenty-eight days of searching. It had crashed on the western slope of the Egan Mountain Range, about ten miles west of the town of Cherry Creek and about forty miles north-northwest of Ely, Nevada. The pilot's remains were found in the cockpit. Officially the primary cause of the accident was undetermined.

Recommendations from the accident report called for all pilots to be rebriefed to ensure they do not fly if they have any doubt about their physical condition. Pilots were also briefed about the correct procedures to follow if they become lost, especially at night. To further enhance safety, all squadron pilots were reappraised of the importance of abandoning the aircraft at least 10,000 feet above terrain when a suitable emergency landing field is not available. The pilots were told to bail out at night at recommended altitudes and not to attempt a flame out landings except at known fields under very favorable conditions. Other recommendations included strengthening the seat structure and relocating the liquid oxygen converter in the cockpit.

The Crash Site Today

At Lt. Bacon's crash site, we spent several hours exploring and carefully examining the wreckage. The wreck is laid out pointing uphill and there is a trail of debris from its impact point below.

Both wings of the F-100 were separated from the fuselage and "USAF" can be read on the upper wing. The national insignia on the lower side is in good condition as it is protected from the elements.

The forward section of the Super Sabre was completely burned. The vertical tail had been cut off and there were torch marks on several other pieces from attempts at salvaging the jet's carcass for the aluminum's melt value. The Pratt & Whitney J57 engine was relatively intact and by examining the inside of the engine, it appeared that it was not running at the time of impact. The jet must have glided until it impacted the mountain.

A couple of binder rings were found. They must have contained the flight logs, maps, and check lists from the pilot. They were vivid reminders of the personal tragedy that took place.

Before leaving we paid our respects at the crash site and left two American flags attached to the wreckage. One located near the cockpit section of the aircraft in memory of the pilot, Lt. Samuel Bacon. Another flag was placed as high as we could near the top of the wreckage for the spirit of Samuel Bacon. He served his country well and he loved what he was doing. May his spirit live on and fly high.

Answering the Questions

By researching this accident and visiting the crash site, I tried to answer a few questions about the plane wreck to dispel some of the myths and legends surrounding it.

Why did the plane crash? High altitude flight, mixed with the pilot's viral illness and possible oxygen/pressurization system failure most likely led to his erratic behavior, hypoxia, and death. An oxygen/pressurization system failure causing hypoxia was not uncommon at that time. The pilot had reported fumes in the cockpit and selected the RAM OFF – PRESSURE OFF position on his cockpit pressurization selector. Hypoxia was suspected due to his erratic actions and slow communications with other members of the flight. The F-100 required pilots to be on 100 percent oxygen all the time because of possible fumes in the cockpit. The liquid oxygen system used a pressure-demand mask and a converter to provide the pilot with breathable oxygen. The jet was flying at over 30,000 feet and, without oxygen, the pilot would have quickly blacked out.

How did the jet get onto the side of the Nevada mountain? Did the pilot attempt to land it there? By viewing its location, it was obvious that this was no place to land a plane. By flying a little further, Bacon would have been over wide open valleys that may have offered a much better place for a forced landing. Pilots in the F-100 Super Sabre were trained to never stay with the jet if they encountered a problem. The procedures required pilots to eject, especially at night over unfamiliar terrain. The crash looks like a survivable accident, but the pilot must have been unconscious, incapacitated, or dead at the time of the crash. With the pilot unconscious, the jet plane would simply fly on autopilot until it ran out of fuel. This would explain why the jet was so far off course. The evidence at the scene confirmed that the engine was not turning at the time of impact and that it most likely flamed out due to fuel starvation. The jet simply fell from the sky after it ran out of fuel, most likely in a flat spin and landed itself. The fuselage skidded up the mountain to its final resting place.

One of the mysteries is why the cockpit section burned after it had apparently completely run out of fuel? According to the accident report there was a failure of the structures securing the seat to the plane, which allowed the seat to slide forward and to the left. It ruptured the liquid oxygen converter and the escaping oxygen increased the intensity of the cockpit fire.

Why is the aircraft in its current condition? It appeared that decades ago someone attempted to salvage and scrap parts from the wreck. The vertical tail was cut off and is missing. Torch marks remain where an unsuccessfully attempt was made to cut up the remainder of the wreck. One wing had a torch cut through the top, but the cut did not get through the main structure. There is an ore car track under one wing most likely used as a leverage bar. Several other parts had torch marks from attempted salvage operations before the scrapper gave up.

A Fitting Tribute

Why are people so intrigued by abandoned things and wrecked planes? Making the journey to the town and crash site was like making a pilgrimage to a sacred monument and opening a time capsule that offered a chance to connect with the past in a direct way. The past is revisited through relics. Cherry Creek is a relic of the old days of the west and the F-100 Super Sabre jet wreck is a relic from aviation history. These two very different relics symbolize freedom, the freedom of the Old West and the freedom won in air battles. The weathered relics remain as reminders of their historic roles in the nation's past and can still be appreciated. History needs to be explored before it drifts into eternity.

I contacted the sister of Samuel "Ken" Bacon. She was only six years old at the time, but she still has vivid memories of the events surrounding her brother's loss. She said that every year her brother Ken is honored by the Brigham Young University Air Force Reserve Officer Training Corps during the Ken Bacon Speech Contest, recognizing his leadership. The information and photos that I sent helped fill in missing information about her brother's loss.

Before leaving Cherry Creek, I donated a binder with a copy of the official accident report, photos, and stories to the town museum. The family of Samuel Bacon and the people of Cherry Creek now know the truth about "The Legend of Airplane Canyon."

David Trojan with memorial flags placed at the crash site. (Dave McCurry)

Wreckage of the NASA Convair 990 and Navy P-3C together on the Sunnyvale Municipal Golf course. The tail of the Convair is in the foreground, while the tail of the P-3C is recognizable at the far side of the wreckage. (NASA)

Chapter 13

Moffett Field Mid-Air: Collision on Final Approach

Ian Abbott

Naval Air Station Moffett Field, located thirty miles south of San Francisco, California, was a busy facility in 1973. The air station was the headquarters for all United States Navy patrol activity in the Pacific, and in this role it was home to many patrol squadrons flying the Lockheed P-3 Orion. Moffett Field was also home to NASA's Ames Research Center, which operated a wide variety of research and experimental aircraft at that time. On April 12, 1973, a Navy Lockheed P-3C and a Convair 990 operated by NASA collided while on final approach to Moffett Field, killing sixteen of the seventeen people aboard the two aircraft.

The Navy P-3C, Buno. 157332, was assigned to Patrol Squadron FOUR SEVEN (VP-47). It had departed Moffett Field for a training flight approximately five and one-half hours prior to the accident. Lt. Stephen A. Schwarting was in command of the P-3, along with two pilots in training, a flight engineer, and two observers. Lt. Schwarting had been a naval aviator for five years and, at age twenty-nine, had logged 2,014 flight hours, 1,014 of those in P-3 aircraft.

During the first part of the training flight, the P-3 operated over the ocean off of Big Sur, California, approximately one hundred miles south of the naval air station. The P-3 and its crew then returned to Moffett Field to practice approaches and landings. At the time of the accident, the P-3 crew had been flying approaches to touch-and-go landings on runway 32L for about ninety minutes, circling in a left-hand pattern west of the air station. There are two parallel runways at Moffett Field, 32L and 32R. Only the right runway was equipped for instrument approaches, but on the day of this collision the weather was fair and the visibility was excellent.

NASA Convair 990, similar to NASA 711 Galileo, *which collided with a Moffett Field-based P-3 Orion over the Sunnyvale Golf Course. (NASA)*

While the P-3 was flying approaches on runway 32L, the NASA Convair 990 was south of Moffett Field flying a straight-in approach. The Convair 990 was a flying laboratory, called *Galileo*, which flew in support of the scientific programs at the Ames Research Center. The Convair 990, N711NA, was delivered to NASA in 1964 and was one of four 990 models operated by the space agency over the years.

On the day of the accident, *Galileo* was returning from a two-hour flight over Monterey Bay to test a newly installed system for surveying migratory sea mammals. In past experiments *Galileo* had chased the 1967 solar eclipse, it had taken astronomers aloft to study comets, and it had last been used in a joint Soviet-American survey of the Bering Sea. *Galileo*'s pilot was James P. Riley, age twenty-eight. There were a total of eleven men aboard the Convair jet, seven were NASA employees, and two employees each were from Teledyne, Inc. and Northrop, Inc.

Galileo's pilot first contacted the Moffett Field tower at 2:46 p.m. local time, reporting that he was ten miles south of the air station and requesting a straight-in approach. At that time, the air traffic controller instructed *Galileo*'s pilot to approach runway 32R and to contact the tower when he was seven miles south of the air field. There were other aircraft in the pattern at the time, and shortly after his exchange with *Galileo* the controller told another aircraft that there were "numerous P-3s left traffic for runway 32."

At 2:48, the pilot of the P-3 contacted the tower reporting that he was "turning base, wheels down, touch and go." The controller acknowledged that transmission and instructed the pilot to "continue for the left side." Seconds later, *Galileo*'s pilot contacted the controller and stated that he was seven miles south of the air station. The controller acknowledged the transmission and, after an exchange with another aircraft, instructed *Galileo*'s pilot to "continue for the right side."

At 2:49, *Galileo*'s pilot contacted the tower and said: "gear down and locked." The controller replied by informing the pilot of the wind speed and direction, and then without explanation he stated that *Galileo* was "cleared to land 32L." *Galileo*'s pilot did not question the change in runway clearance, but acknowledged it by stating

"32L, thank you." A few moments later the air traffic control transcript contains a transmission that is probably from Lt. Schwarting's P-3, stating "…touch and go on left side." The tower acknowledged this transmission by instructing the P-3 to "continue." At this point the two aircraft began to converge on the left runway approach.

At 2:50, the air traffic control transcript contains an unidentified transmission, "Tower, you got that" followed by a second, garbled transmission. The controller replied to these two transmissions by saying "go around, go around we've…" The controller then transmitted the instruction "all aircraft in the pattern climb and maintain 1,500." By that time *Galileo* and the P-3 had collided and crashed together about one-half mile south of the runway.

At the time of the collision *Galileo* was apparently above the P-3, descending on a converging path. According to the official Navy investigation, the fuselage at the base of the P-3's vertical stabilizer showed evidence of two tire marks that matched *Galileo*'s dual nose gear tires. In addition, three pieces of the P-3's fuselage were found embedded in *Galileo*'s nose gear.

According to eyewitnesses, the P-3 pulled up sharply in the moment before the collision, perhaps in evasive action. *Galileo* struck the upper aft fuselage of the P-3 and the two aircraft fell, entangled, onto the twelfth tee of the Sunnyvale Municipal Golf Course. A large fire immediately engulfed the two wrecked aircraft. Although there were people playing golf nearby, no one on the ground was hurt.

The crash scene quickly became chaotic. The two aircraft crashed just 200 yards from the Bayshore Freeway, and drivers left their cars to scale the fence and rush to the burning wreckage. Golfers, and people from nearby office buildings who had seen the crash, also swarmed around the site. The large number of onlookers made access

P-3 Orion maritime patrol planes line the Moffett Field ramp with historic Hangar One in the background. At the time of the accident, Moffett Field was the West Coast headquarters for anti-submarine warfare training. (U.S. Navy)

Fire fighters extinguish the flames in the wreckage of the Galileo and prepare to recover the remains of the crew. (NASA Ames Research Center)

Fire fighters and rescue personnel from Moffett Field and the adjacent cities of Sunnyvale and Mountain View responded to the crash. (NASA Ames Research Center)

An illustration of the tangled mess that was the aftermath of the midair: Galileo's fuselage rests on its port side with one of the P-3's Allison turbo-prop engines is at the right foreground.

Emergency vehicles remain around the wreckage after the post-crash fire has been extinguished. There were no casualties involving non-aircrew people on the ground, but the wreckage fell just yards away from the busy freeway that separates the golf course from Moffett Field. (NASA Ames Research Center)

difficult for the fire crews responding from Moffett Field and Sunnyvale. At the time of the crash a group of firemen were watching a demonstration of a "jaws of life" rescue device at the Mountain View Fire Department training center. When they saw the crash they loaded the rescue equipment and went to the scene, hoping that they could assist.

Sixteen men died in the crash or in the subsequent fire. The sole survivor was Petty Officer Third Class Bruce N. Mallibert, who was an observer aboard the P-3. One of the golfers at the crash scene found Mallibert seriously injured and lying unconscious outside of the wreckage. He mistakenly thought that Mallibert was dead, and he covered Mallibert's body with a parachute.

Mallibert was lucky to have survived the crash, but he escaped death a second time minutes later. A fire truck drove over the parachute, its driver unaware that Mallibert was underneath it. Miraculously, the truck's wheels missed Mallibert on both sides. Soon after, a fireman found Mallibert and discovered that he was still alive. He was taken to a nearby hospital where he remained in critical condition for many days.

This crash renewed calls for the Navy to leave Moffett Field. Several local members of Congress called for a halt to flying from Moffett Field in the days following the crash. There had been a large number of crashes around the air station when fighters and attack aircraft were based there in the 1950s, but P-3 operations had an excellent safety record. This collision was the only crash involving a P-3 near the airfield between the early 1960s, when patrol operations began, and 1994, when the Navy decommissioned Naval Air Station Moffett Field.

With the *Galileo* accident, NASA lost a unique research asset in addition to several of the scientists who had helped to develop the flying laboratory and its experiments. Many of the programs that were to use *Galileo* were either delayed for years or were cancelled following the crash.

Today, Moffett Field is officially designated Moffett Federal Airfield. The Navy is gone, but the California Air National Guard's 129th Rescue Wing is stationed there and other military and government aircraft use the field occasionally. NASA eventually transferred all of the aircraft that had been operated by the Ames Research Center to what is now the Armstrong Flight Research Center at Edwards Air Force Base. There is far less traffic at Moffett Field today than there was in 1973.

The final approaches to runways 32L and 32R still pass over the Sunnyvale Municipal Golf Course. There is no evidence on the course of the tragic mid-air collision that took place more than forty-five years ago.

This accident apparently occurred because of a simple mistake in air traffic control procedures. The weather was excellent, no mechanical or electronic failures were involved, and the crews on board each aircraft were well trained and experienced. Sixteen men and two valuable aircraft were lost, but future accidents may have been prevented through enhanced awareness of Moffett Field's particular operations.

The mass of metal that was Lt. Stephen A. Schwarting's P-3 Orion from Patrol Squadron 47 lies on the Sunnyvale Golf Course while first responders comb through the wreckage. (NASA Ames Research Center)

Although the two aircraft were headed for the same runway, the wreckage came to rest oriented in opposite directions. Here the cockpit of Galileo can be seen beside the tail of the P-3C. This was the only serious accident involving the P-3 on or around Moffett Field during more than 25 years of operations. (NASA Ames Research Center)

Turkish Airlines DC-10-10 TC-JAV, msn 46704, crashed on March 3, 1974, near Senlis, France. The crash took 346 lives and sparked a controversy over the design of the DC-10's cargo-door locking mechanism. TC-JAV had reached 11,000 feet when a cargo compartment door blew out, decompressing the cabin, which resulted in the structural failure of the cabin floor. Cables to the Number Two powerplant, elevator, and rudder are assumed to have been disabled, causing a steep rate of descent, from which the crew was unable to recover. (ATP/Airliners America)

Chapter 14

Paris Departure Disaster: Turkish DC-10 Ankara

Ian Abbott

In the early 1970s, the first generation of long-range commercial jet transports gave way to the new "wide body" airliners. The Boeing Company's 747 entered commercial service first, but the McDonnell Douglas Corporation's DC-10 was close behind when it first carried passengers in 1971. The new DC-10 dwarfed its predecessor, the DC-8, and its sheer size magnified the challenges faced by McDonnell Douglas engineers.

There were weaknesses in the DC-10's initial design. Some of those weaknesses would first make themselves known in a terrifying incident in 1972. Twenty months later, in 1974, the weaknesses would cause an air disaster in Paris that was the greatest loss of life to date.

The Design

As originally designed, the latching mechanism on the DC-10's rear cargo door could appear to be secure when, in fact, it was not properly locked. At altitude, the interior of the aircraft was pressurized, while the air pressure outside was much lower. This pressure difference could produce enough force to open the rear cargo door if not properly locked.

If the cargo door opened at altitude, the cargo compartment would quickly depressurize, while higher air pressure remained in the passenger cabin. The floor of the passenger cabin would be subjected to a tremendous load until the pressure equalized. Vents were designed to allow air to flow from the passenger cabin into the cargo compartment, relieving the load on the floor. These vents, however, were inadequate.

Sign pointing toward the crash memorial in the Foret d'Ermenonville. (Ian E. Abbott)

These walls form the right and left panels of the memorial on which the names of crew members and passengers are recorded. (Ian E. Abbott)

Following a failure of the cargo door at altitude, and as a result of the insufficient venting between the passenger cabin and the cargo compartment, the higher pressure in the passenger cabin could cause parts of the cabin floor to collapse. The control cables for the rudder and elevators on the DC-10 ran through the floor structure, so damage to the floor could compromise or disable the control cables. This last aspect of the DC-10 design could therefore allow a chain of events starting with a locking problem in the cargo door and ending with an almost total loss of control.

Windsor and the "Gentleman's Agreement"

A rear cargo door failure took place during American Airlines Flight 96 on June 11, 1972. The aircraft, registered N103AA (c/n 46503), was flying from Detroit to New York's La Guardia Airport with fifty-six passengers and a crew of eleven onboard. Captain Bryce McCormick was in command, assisted by First Officer (F/O) Peter Paige-Whitney and Second Officer (S/O) Clayton Burke.

Flight 96 was late departing Detroit, with some of the delay due to difficulty in locking the rear cargo door. There were problems with locking this door in the past, but the ground crew at Detroit finally decided that the door was securely fastened and N103AA took off.

Passing through 12,000 feet over Windsor, Ontario, a loud noise from the rear of the aircraft startled everyone on board. In the cabin, moisture condensed momentarily into fog as air rushed suddenly toward the rear of the plane. Captain McCormick and F/O Paige-Whitney felt the rudder pedals jerk as air rushing through the cockpit swirled dust and grit around them.

The rear cargo door that appeared secure prior to takeoff had opened. The difference in pressure between the passenger cabin and the rear cargo compartment caused the floor of the lounge area in the rear of the aircraft to collapse. This, in turn, damaged the control cables running through the floor. The crew declared an emergency and after assessing their reduced control of the aircraft, turned back to Detroit.

Captain McCormick and his crew had to vary the thrust settings of the wing-mounted engines to help control pitch and rate of descent. Damage to the rudder controls meant that the aircraft yawed considerably during landing at Detroit. The flight crew displayed excellent airmanship, but only luck prevented a catastrophic loss of control.

The National Transportation Safety Board (NTSB) had little trouble in determining the initial cause of the incident over Windsor. Marks on the cargo door latches clearly showed that the latches had not been properly locked. When the ground crew at Detroit pushed down on the door handle, it should have positioned a locking pin behind a restraining flange on each door latch.

The latches were not fully closed, however, and the locking pins jammed against the sides of the restraining flanges. Flexibility in the torque tube that operated the mechanism allowed the handle to close anyway, giving the impression that the door was properly locked when it was not. As the aircraft climbed, the pressure difference between the inside of the aircraft and the outside air increased. The cargo door was forced open because its locking pins were not behind the restraining flanges. As a result, a plane and its passengers were brought to the brink of disaster.

McDonnell Douglas and the contractor that manufactured the door, Convair, were already aware that there were problems with the design. Before the Windsor incident, McDonnell Douglas had received approximately one hundred reports of problems with the cargo door from airlines operating the DC-10.

Shortly after the Windsor incident, the NTSB recommended that the Federal Aviation Administration (FAA) issue an Airworthiness Directive requiring that every DC-10 have its cargo door modified. These modifications would have been made at McDonnell Douglas' expense.

The FAA, however, declined to issue an Airworthiness Directive. Instead, FAA officials made a "gentleman's agreement" with McDonnell Douglas management. Under this agreement, McDonnell Douglas would issue service bulletins to DC-10 operators recommending changes to the doors, and the changes would be incorporated on all future DC-10 aircraft. The bulletins recommended installation of a support plate to prevent distortion of the torque tube that operated the locking pins, as well as an adjustment to the locking pins that would dramatically increase the amount of force required to lock the door properly.

Turkish Airlines took delivery of three DC-10s in December 1972. One of these aircraft (msn 46704) was given the Turkish registration TC-JAV and was named *Ankara*. TC-JAV was the twenty-ninth DC-10 produced, and since it was delivered after McDonnell Douglas issued the service bulletins in response to the Windsor incident, the modification should have been incorporated.

The assembly and inspection of each aircraft in Long Beach, California, was supposed to be carefully documented, and the paperwork

The central pillar of the memorial's engraving reads "In memory of the victims of the great air disaster..." (Ian E. Abbott)

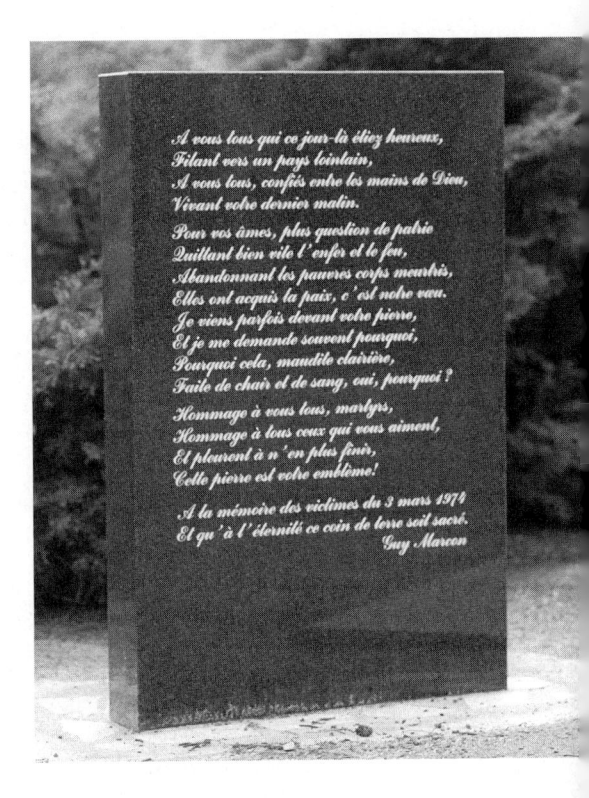

Poem at the memorial which concludes: "In memory of the victims of March 3, 1974 / And may this corner of the earth be sacred forever." (Ian E. Abbott)

Trees were planted in regular rows to replace the forest cleared away by the crash of TC-JAV. (Ian E. Abbott)

for the twenty-ninth DC-10 indicated that its cargo door was built to the latest specifications. Actually, the support plate that was to have been added to prevent distortion of the torque tube was not installed on the assembly line. The responsible inspector was later identified and removed from his position, but this discrepancy would contribute to the jetliner's final fate. That mistake was compounded in the weeks leading up to Flight 981 when the locking pins on TC-JAV were improperly adjusted.

McDonnell Douglas had issued a service bulletin suggesting that the locking pins be adjusted to increase their travel. The recommended adjustment would have significantly increased the amount of force required to close the locking handle if the locking pins were not behind the restraining flanges. Instead, Turkish Airlines mechanics had decreased the locking pin travel, which actually reduced the amount of force required to close the locking handle properly. Together, these factors allowed the baggage handler to easily close the locking handle when the locking pins were not behind their restraining flanges.

Leather shoe sole found at crash site. (Ian E. Abbott)

The Accident

Orly Airport outside of Paris was extremely busy on Sunday, March 3, 1974. A strike by ground workers at London's Heathrow Airport had caused all British European Airways and Air France flights from Paris to London to be cancelled. The terminal was full of travelers trying to get to London on any other available airline flight. Turkish Airlines Flight 981 had seats available for its afternoon flight to London, so many passengers who had originally made other plans purchased tickets at the Turkish Airlines counter.

A diverse group of passengers boarded Flight 981. Tom Wright, a U.S. citizen employed by Merrill Lynch in London, and his wife Fay were returning from a weekend trip to the continent. British nationals boarding the DC-10 included all eighteen members of the Bury-St. Edmonds Rugby Club, whose exhibition game that day had been cancelled. The athletes were among almost 200 British passengers aboard Flight 981. Thirty-eight Japanese citizens also boarded TC-JAV. Many were recent university graduates taking a world tour before beginning what promised to be a lifetime of work at prestigious Japanese corporations. Among the Japanese were a newly married couple, Atsuko and Takehiro Higuchi, who were on their honeymoon.

TC-JAV landed at 11:02 a.m. local time, arriving from Istanbul. Employees of Samor, an airport service company, unloaded the baggage of passengers staying in Paris and prepared to load the baggage of those now joining the flight to London. Samor employees emptied the DC-10's rear cargo compartment. An employee named Mohamed Mahmoudi was responsible for securing the rear cargo compartment door. He would later say that he noticed nothing unusual as he pushed the locking handle down flush with the skin of the aircraft at 11:35 a.m.

The flight crew aboard TC-JAV included Captain Nejat Berkoz, F/O Oral Ulusman, and S/O Erhan Ozer. A total of 334 passengers and twelve crew were aboard TC-JAV when it was pushed back from the terminal gate at 12:20 p.m. Flight 981 began its takeoff roll at 12:31 p.m. At 12:34 the crew reported to Paris air traffic controllers that they were passing through 6,000 feet. At 12:36 the crew received clearance to climb to 23,000 feet.

According to noises on the cockpit voice recorder, the rear cargo door opened at 12:39:56 as the aircraft climbed through 13,000 feet. When the door locking mechanism failed, the higher air pressure in the passenger cabin caused the floor near the cargo door opening to collapse. Two rows of seats, carrying a total of six passengers, were torn from the aircraft and fell near the town of St. Pathus, France. The bodies of the passengers in their seats landed near the cargo door in a plowed field.

Seventy-seven seconds after the rear cargo door opened, the image of Flight 981 disappeared from Paris air traffic control radar displays. Immediately after the door opened and the cabin floor collapsed, the aircraft pitched down and began to yaw to the left. As the dive angle increased so did the airspeed, setting off alarms in the cockpit. The flight crew struggled to understand what had happened and attempted to regain control. Captain Berkoz added power and by doing so reduced the angle of descent. The aircraft had lost too much altitude, however, and at 12:41:13 Flight 981 crashed in a forested area with its left wing down and the nose only slightly below level. The airspeed at impact was nearly 500 mph, and in a matter of seconds the aircraft disintegrated as it continued almost a half mile through the trees.

All 346 people onboard the aircraft were killed. Grieving relatives traveled to Paris from around the world and French authorities devoted their finest forensic resources to identifying remains. The Paris crash would remain the worst in aviation history until the collision between two Boeing 747s at Tenerife in 1976.

Largest piece of aircraft seen by the author at the crash site. (Ian E. Abbott)

The Crash Site

During a trip to France, my wife and I were in Paris and decided to visit the crash site of Flight 981. We knew that a monument was built where the aircraft crashed in the *Foret d' Ermenonville* (Ermenonville Forest), northeast of Charles de Gaulle Airport. We purchased a roadmap of the Ile de France region and saw that the *Foret d' Ermenonville* was public land, similar to a national forest in the United States.

We took a train from the Gare du Nord station in Paris to Charles de Gaulle Airport. I do not speak French, but with the help of a phrasebook, the roadmap, and a note with the date of the crash we were able to find a taxi driver who was willing to try to find the site. Our taxi driver stopped several times to ask local people for directions to the crash site.

The last, crucial set of directions came from a group of bicyclists, and soon we were driving down a one-lane dirt road that led about a half mile into the forest from the paved road. There was a clearing at the end of the dirt road where a few other cars were parked.

Several trails led away from the clearing and a small sign that read *Memorial de la Catastrophe Aerienne* was posted near one. We negotiated with the taxi driver to wait for one hour. It had taken more than a half hour to drive from the airport and we certainly didn't want to walk back.

The sky was overcast as we walked through the forest and the only sounds other than our footsteps were the wind blowing through the trees and crows calling overhead. Several hundred yards down the trail we had our first view of the monument. We were alone as we stood at the edge of a small clearing dominated by a rough-hewn column of granite and two long, black granite walls with the names of the victims engraved upon them. Our sense of the number of people who had lost their lives here was amplified by seeing each of their names, column after column, engraved on the walls. A memorial poem, in French, is engraved upon a fourth slab of black granite.

Previous visitors had placed pieces of wreckage at the base of the column. Some of the pieces evoked the fate of the passengers, particularly a partially burned, yellow

Small pieces of wreckage placed on the base of the central pillar of the memorial. (Ian E. Abbott)

plastic oxygen mask. There were also pieces of upholstery and carpet that were quite recognizable despite being dirty and faded.

The trees around the monument are of random types and sizes, but as we walked farther into the forest we noticed that the trees became uniform. These were pine trees planted after the crash to cover the long swath cut by the aircraft as it disintegrated.

Although decades had passed since the crash, and despite the fact that a major cleanup effort had occurred, there was still a significant amount of wreckage scattered among the younger trees. There was very little brush among the trees and it was easy to walk in any direction. We could not walk more than a few yards without seeing a piece of wreckage.

Most of the pieces were small; shredded aluminum, bits of wire and cable, and scraps of carpet. Among the recognizable pieces I found were an overhead reading light assembly and a piece of a laminated serving tray, complete with indentations where drinking glasses would have been placed. We also found two pieces of shoes, a rubber heel and a leather inner sole, which seemed particularly personal lying among the metal and plastic that had been an airplane.

The one large piece of wreckage we saw was a heavy assembly about five feet long and two feet wide. I could not determine what it had been, but its torn metal and sheared rivets testified to the force of the crash.

Finally, it was time to turn back down the trail to our taxi for the trip back to the airport. We walked by the monument one more time, stopping beneath the gray sky to contemplate the chapter of aviation history that was written here. We knew that Flight 981 was a great tragedy, but its magnitude wasn't comprehensible until we stood at the crash site.

After the Paris crash the problems with the DC-10 cargo door were decisively addressed and DC-10s carried millions of passengers safely. Today, the DC-10 has disappeared from passenger service, replaced by newer designs. We can only hope that the unfortunate combination of engineering, politics, and human error that produced this accident will never be repeated.

The accident aircraft, N110AA, shown being towed at SFO (the San Mateo bridge is visible just beneath the rear fuselage). Although the NTSB found maintenance to blame, generally N110AA was not a poorly maintained aircraft. Thirty-seven Airworthiness Directives issued for the DC-10 applicable to N110AA and six issued for the engine installation had all been complied with. Maintenance was also performed an optional Service Bulletin. (Airliners/ATP)

Chapter 15

Point of No Return: The Crash of American Air Lines Flight 191 Heavy

Michael H. Marlow

On March 1, 1962, Mr. and Mrs. Julius Stogel of Brooklyn, New York, boarded Los Angeles-bound American Airlines Flight 1 at New York International Airport, then called Idlewild. It was a beautiful day for flying, the skies were clear with visibility fifteen miles and twenty mph winds. Taking off to the northwest, less than two minutes later, a sudden rudder problem caused the Boeing 707 to roll to the left and dive, inverted, into Jamaica Bay, "...as if something reached up from the earth, grabbed its nose and pulled it down." The Stogels and all ninety-three others aboard died. At the time it was the worst U.S. commercial plane crash involving a single aircraft.

Seventeen years later, their son Leonard, 44 and the father of two, boarded Flight 191, a Los Angeles-bound American Airlines flight at Chicago O'Hare International Airport. It was also a beautiful day for flying, with clear skies, visibility 15 miles, and a strong 22 mph wind. Operating a McDonnell Douglas Corp. DC-10-10, Flight 191 lifted off the runway into the northwest, but 30 seconds later, the aircraft rolled to the left and dove, inverted, into a field. Leonard Stogel and 270 others aboard the jetliner, plus two on the ground, died. Flight 191 became the deadliest U.S. commercial plane crash.

The story of American Airlines Flight 191 is one of coincidence, irony, and tragedy. There are tales of good fortune and bad, as well as accounts of luck in many different shades. It is the story of passengers who knew more about their aircraft at the critical moments than the pilots who were flying it. It is also the story of capable pilots who were struggling to right their jetliner as it rolled out of control, yet died not knowing what went wrong–of an airliner that gave seven years of sterling service, then suddenly turned deadly in the worst possible way. It's the story of two people who

Flight 191 taxies to Runway 32R – and into aviation history. This photo was taken just before 3 p.m., on May 25, 1979. Less than ten minutes later, this aircraft and its 271 occupants would cease to exist. American Airlines could not have placed a more competent flight crew in the front office of N110AA. The combined 4,800 hours of DC-10 experience was defeated by a chain of events and circumstances that would have overcome any flight crew. It was also a series of events and circumstances that sank the Titanic and caused the worst commercial plane crash in history – the collision in 1977 of two Boeing 747s on a runway at Tenerife, in the Canary Islands. (Jon Proctor Collection)

performed acts of kindness, acts that saved one of their lives but took the other's. This true story reads like fiction.

It was an unspeakably malevolent gathering of small, insidious errors that overtook a mighty airplane and the trained and dedicated workers who flew and maintained it. Within a short time, the entire domestic fleet of the aircraft type would be grounded, and the foreign ones prohibited from U.S. airspace. Its manufacturer, a pioneer of commercial aviation, would be shaken to its foundation and would never fully recover.

Prelude to Disaster

The seeds of the impending tragedy were planted two months earlier at a maintenance facility in Tulsa, Oklahoma. American's mechanics had removed and then reinstalled the plane's engine and pylon, the part which attaches the engine to the wing, as one unit instead of individually as McDonnell Douglas, the plane's manufacturer, recommended. Utilizing a forklift, it was a difficult operation at best. Proper alignment and execution were critical and, unless performed flawlessly, could cause unseen damage where the pylon attached to the wing. When first approached with the proposal, the manufacturer's response was that it "would not encourage this procedure due to the element of risk involved in the remating of the combined engine and pylon assembly to the wing attach points." But maintenance personnel felt confident in their revised, time-saving procedure.

This series of important yet tragic images were captured by William Warke, a passenger arriving at O'Hare on board another DC-10. These copyright images are used with Warke's permission.

After losing an engine, Flight 191 continues to climb, apparently effortlessly, on its two remaining engines. The only sign of trouble aside from the missing engine is the trail of hydraulic fluid. The landing gear has not been, nor was it ever, raised. At this point the possibility still existed to save the flight, but only a gut feeling and a deviation from standard emergency procedures without justification (from the pilots' viewpoints) could have done so.

Its ability to maintain flight hanging in the balance, Flight 191 teeters between life and death. The debate continues today among airline pilots as to whether or not the flight was recoverable at this point, even had the pilots been made fully aware of their situation and done everything correctly. Even eyewitnesses unfamiliar with commercial flight recognized that this extreme bank wasn't normal for an airliner.

It's all over. Its fate now sealed, there is nothing that anyone, including the pilots, can do but watch. The terror experienced by those aboard can only begin to be imagined. American's DC-10s were equipped at the time with video cameras in the cockpit that allowed passengers to view their flight from a different perspective. It was intended to be a form of entertainment.

A black, sinister-looking plume of smoke marks where it all ended. The spoilers on William Warke's DC-10 are just starting to deploy.

The ground smolders near the crash site where the skies turned from blue to black as firefighters from O'Hare, Chicago, and many surrounding suburbs battled the fires. Due to a lack of nearby hydrants, some lines had to be run for over half a mile. This created a problem at first, as Chicago's fire hoses used a different coupling than their suburban counterparts. Fortunately, some suburban fire departments carried special adapters. News media has already arrived, evidenced by the cameraman on top of the news truck at right.

In the background on this photo is Runway 32R from which 191 made its takeoff, behind it the Chicago skyline. Touhy Avenue is clearly visible, with the canine training center in the center of the photo. The dark streak in the left center is the trough carved out by the left wing, and dominating the bottom of the photo is the mobile home park. The large building at lower left is the MC Steel Co. building.

The Fatal Flight

The tragic consequences would come to pass on May 25, 1979. American Flight 191 departed Gate K-5, lined up on O'Hare's Runway 32R, and received clearance for takeoff at about 3:03 p.m. local time. Eight seconds later, as the silver DC-10 released brakes and started barreling down the runway, Captain Walter H. Lux radioed the final transmission from the flight: "American 191 under way."

It was supposed to be just another routine flight as the massive DC-10 started its takeoff run. Everything appeared normal as the aircraft passed through V1, the speed at which the aircraft became committed to flight regardless of any emergency. Until that moment, Flight 191 was just another 380,000 pounds of aluminum, jet fuel, and people thundering down the 10,000-foot-long runway. Then, at that magical moment known as "rotation," when the nose gently lifted and the jetliner floated off the runway and entered the domain for which it was built, something went terribly wrong.

The first sign of trouble was a "thud" heard on the flight deck. Suddenly, some of the captain's instruments went dead; others indicated a failure of the engine on the left wing, known as the "number one" engine. More a nuisance than anything, it was a situation for which the flight crew was well trained. After all, they had practiced handling engine failures hundreds of times in a flight simulator. It was something their combined experience of 46,800 flight hours could easily handle. They were well paid for their expertise. But they were not in a flight simulator and things were not as they seemed.

As trained, the flight crew began engine-out procedures and pulled the nose of the aircraft up even further, causing the aircraft to decelerate. As the procedure mandated, they needed to reach obstacle clearance or 800 feet, whichever was higher, before they could level out to increase speed. Passing through 300 feet and already well above any obstacles, they were waiting to reach 800 feet.

They would never reach that altitude.

At 325 feet, the aircraft behaved in a manner that puzzled them as it started to roll to the left. Faced with a myriad of warning lights indicating multiple system failures, the pilots had scant seconds to evaluate, prioritize, and take action. The first officer, flying the aircraft with some functioning instruments, responded properly. But the aircraft wouldn't stop. It kept rolling over on its left wing past the vertical, started to roll on its back, shuddered, and nosed down. Never giving up, the determined copilot kept applying full opposite aileron and rudder controls until impact, in a final, desperate attempt to avoid the inevitable. As the massive DC-10 fell lazily towards the ground, the pilots could only watch, helpless and stunned, as the ground rushed at them in full view through the DC-10's panoramic view windscreen. Their flight, intended to last four hours, lasted only thirty-one seconds. It ended by plunging into a field, creating an intense fireball as 80,000 pounds of fuel ignited.

They perished never knowing why. Why did the aircraft roll? Why didn't it respond to the flight controls? Why didn't stall warnings go off?

What Happened?

As the world shot past them at 180 mph, passengers seated near the left windows saw important things the flight crew could not, images that might have allowed the pilots to save the flight. What they saw was 13,477 pounds of engine and pylon suddenly break loose and vault over the wing. They saw the result—a three-foot gash sliced in the

The trough made by the left wing was two feet deep and about 100 feet long. The unburned grass is testimony to the aircraft's westerly direction and strong tailwind at the time of impact. When viewed from directly above the scorched earth took the shape of a pie wedge.

Although filled in, years of settling have caused the trough to reappear as a slight depression. After a heavy rainfall or when the snow melts in the spring (when this photo was taken) puddles form to mark its location.

leading edge of the wing and, most critical of all, precious hydraulic fluid pouring out. It was the DC-10's equivalent of having a wrist slashed. Passengers watched helplessly through small windows as the aircraft's lifeblood drained out before their eyes.

Losing hydraulic fluid crippled the jetliner. Without mechanical locking devices, only hydraulic pressure kept the leading-edge slats extended. Leading-edge slats are panels at the front edge of the wing. The slats are deployed during takeoffs and landings, and are critical to the aircraft's performance during those times.

As the fluid bled out, the outboard leading-edge slats collapsed back into the wing, resulting in a loss of lift on the left wing, causing it to stall and drop as the aircraft decelerated. The speed needed to keep the damaged left wing flying had, unknown to the pilots, been dramatically increased. Ironically, the aircraft's deceleration was the result of the implementation of standard emergency procedures. What was in reality a stall and roll was perceived by the pilots to be just a roll, to which they responded accordingly. It was a stall from which they could not recover.

What nobody could see was the disabling of crucial warning systems as the departing pylon severed lines. The slat disagreement warning system was rendered inoperative. So was the stall warning system; it lost power that moments earlier had been supplied by the engine that now lay on the runway behind them.

Even the "natural" stall warning system, in the form of shuddering, was denied the pilots. Because the left inboard leading-edge slats remained extended, the aerodynamics became such that little, if any, buffeting was generated. The shuddering may have been mistaken for, or hidden, by turbulence.

By a cruel fate, several company mechanics getting off work would witness the tragedy. Pride would turn to concern and just as quickly to horror as the shiny DC-10 would, in the space of less than a minute, go from being a proud member of their fleet to a perilously damaged jetliner and finally, to a charred and obliterated wreck..

Close Call

Flight 191 impacted at the site of the former Ravenswood Airport in Elk Grove Village, and a mere one hundred yards from the edge of the Touhy Mobile Home Park. It was less than one-half mile from an Amoco fuel storage facility on the other side of the park. The DC-10 came down in one of the few open areas in the densely populated region surrounding O'Hare Airport. Even so, it narrowly missed the trailer park where 1,000 people were living. Still, flying debris and flames destroyed a mobile home and several businesses at the abandoned airport.

When the DC-10 struck the ground, the force from the resulting explosion could be felt for hundreds of yards. A service station on nearby Touhy Avenue had its windows blown out. A homeowner said his mobile home was, "picked up like a cracker box and set down again." A trough two feet deep and one hundred feet long was created by the left wing's impact. Farthest from the point of impact was a piece of the fuselage containing a cabin door. It landed on one of the streets in the mobile home park only 725 feet from where the left wing struck. The number one engine lay beside the O'Hare runway barely damaged, as one newspaper reporter phrased it, "...like the drunken driver who always emerges unscathed after causing a fatal car wreck." Langhorne Bond, the Federal Aviation Administration (FAA) chief at the time, spoke of the wrecked DC-10: "It's overwhelming. It's hard to tell there was a DC-10 here. I'm sure the pieces add up to one, but...."

The crash site as it appeared in 1979, before cleanup had begun...

True Professionals

There were ten air traffic controllers working the tower when Flight 191 crashed. The controller monitoring the flight witnessed the entire accident and quickly gained his nine coworkers' attention:

Controller [3:03:39 PM]: *"Look at this…look at this…blew up an engine… equipment…(we) need equipment…he blew an engine…holy…"*

The controller radioed the troubled airliner, "American 191, do you want to come back? If so, what runway do you want?" The only response was silence. Flight 191's pilots were too busy assessing their situation as seconds later, they would be fighting for their very lives. The supervisor immediately went for the red button alerting O'Hare's four fire stations, pushing it before Flight 191 impacted. As controllers gathered, the drama continued to unfold in the loft high above the world's busiest airport:

Controller [3:03:59 PM]: *"He's not talkin' to me…yeah, but he's gonna lose a wing…there he goes! There he goes!!"*

The controllers watched, horrified, as the DC-10 rolled over and fell to the ground, a huge fireball marking the premature end of its flight. A trip meant to cross the country instead barely made it across Touhy Avenue, just north of the airport. Witnessing the crash proved too much for the controller:

Controller [3:04:14 PM]: *"Oh…I need to be relieved…"*

The supervisor switched his attention and closed Runway 32R, now blocked by the engine and other debris. He also closed other runways on the north side of the airport so that any air rescue efforts would not be hampered by air traffic. The southern half of the airport continued flight operations.

Having all witnessed the traumatic event, the emotional and mental well-being of the controllers, and thus air safety, became paramount. An emotionally shaken controller could not be allowed to continue to handle air traffic. The FAA's facility operations officer checked the watch supervisor, who was okay and returned to duty. The others were each taken aside and asked, "Are you okay?" Most responded positively and returned to their stations.

That same scene in March 1998. The destroyed businesses were later replaced by a semi-truck trailer storage lot.

Ground control first heard about the accident from an unidentified voice on the frequency. The conversation began just as the DC-10 left the runway:

[Voice]: *"That airplane just left an engine out here."* [pause, as he watches the DC-10 crash] *Oh my God! Damn! O'Hare tower, this is EZ-2. You know I'm still out here. Did you see that airplane crash, didn't you?"*

[Ground Control]: *"No, but I saw the smoke."*

[Voice]: *"Yeah, there was an airplane crash down here. You better close that runway out of 14-left* (note: This is the same physical runway as 32-right). *There's an engine in the middle of the runway here."*

While the controllers' experience may have been traumatic, that experienced by those on the ground at the crash scene was sheer terror, second only to those aboard the doomed flight itself.

Terror from The Sky

Abe Marmel, 75, never saw it coming. He never heard it. Tending his garden with his back to the plunging airliner, with eerie silence it came up from behind him. Having operated the former Ravenswood Airport, he had worked in O'Hare's shadow for decades and had grown accustomed to the noise. It wasn't until the DC-10 exploded less than a hundred yards away that he realized the danger he was in. Fire and debris rained around him as he ran into his office. He found his wife Shirley, sixty-nine, standing, paralyzed with fear as the rear of the office burst into flames. He yelled to her, "Get Out!" but she remained frozen, petrified by the flames. Grabbing her arm, he led her out to safety.

Marmel owned the ten acres onto which Flight 191 plummeted. His business destroyed, what remained was the sign on Touhy Avenue that advertised it. It had an arrow that pointed to the crashed jetliner, followed by the words, "Airplane Parts, 320 W. Touhy."

Another person wasn't so lucky. Panicking, he ran through a wall of fire trying to escape, emerging from the flames on fire. Fortunately, an ambulance crew a half mile away was returning from a prior call, saw the fireball, and diverted to the scene. They were credited with saving his life, although he sustained severe burns.

Investigators focus their attention on a smaller piece of wreckage while the destroyed hangar and engine number two sit in the background.

Kenneth Burger was the lead trainer at the Chicago Police Department's canine training center. The DC-10's point of impact was less than 200 yards from the center's main building. Burger said he heard alternating engine and "popping" noises, and looked up just in time to see the DC-10's left wing knife into the ground. Standing only one hundred yards from the impact point on the upwind side, he could feel the heat from the resulting explosion. Thinking quickly, he sent two officers to open the front gate so that emergency vehicles could enter. He and another officer then ran into the thick smoke to see if they could render assistance. When they emerged, they looked at each other with puzzled, mirrored expressions: "Where's the plane?" Running back through the smoke and emerging at the north end, all they saw was an engine and main landing gear assembly. It was only then that they realized that there was no plane. What they saw was all that remained of the huge airliner. There was nothing that they, nor anyone else, could do.

Burger described the experience as the most traumatic of his life. Two days after the crash, and not near anything that was at the crash scene, he again smelled the acrid

A smashed LD-3 container reveals the airline victim of this crash. The number stenciled on the container is also, coincidentally, the year the crash occurred. Not everything burned despite the huge fireball, as evidenced by the untouched paper in the foreground.

fumes as he got out of his car after arriving home from work. When he got to the front door, the smell was gone.

Ray Devito watched Flight 191's takeoff from the observation deck (long since closed) but didn't notice the engine tear loose. He did notice the vapor trail but didn't think much of it as the plane disappeared behind a terminal building. He turned to walk away but something made him turn back. "God, it's taking a long time for it to come up from behind that building," he thought. When it finally did emerge, it was sideways – one wing pointed to where it was meant to be, and the other to its ultimate and tragic destination.

He ran almost three miles to the crashed jetliner, crossing two runways and scaling fences in the process. When he reached the crash site, he reacted as did Ken Burger: "Where's the plane? Where's the damn plane?" He drifted about aimlessly, eventually finding himself beside a phone listening to reporters telling editors that there were "no survivors." Their words struck deep–his twenty-one-year-old fiancée was one of Flight 191's passengers.

One of the first persons to reach the crash scene had been driving on the nearby Northwest Tollway when he felt his car shake from the explosion. He later described what he saw: "That plane did a complete nosedive, and the tail of the plane kept heading west after the rest of the fuselage went down. It just tore off and kept going." When he arrived on the scene, he saw amidst the wreckage a child's book. It was titled, "The Beginning of Life."

Where's Flight 191?

In Los Angeles, about thirty people who had not yet heard of Flight 191's demise came to greet the plane at the gate. They were confused by American's initial reaction, which was to remove the flight number from the arrival screen. Realizing that they would inevitably have to deal with grief-stricken relatives, the flight number was returned to the screen but no gate was listed; just the notation "See Agent."

Each relative or friend was escorted to a private room behind American Airlines' Gate 42, where the flight would have disembarked. A priest, who happened to have been at the airport when the tragic news was breaking, comforted them. A physician was also brought in by the airline.

American's employees were also emotionally stressed by the crash. One employee said, "You are really never ready for something like this." When asked how he reacted upon first hearing the news, he responded, "I got sick. I thought I was going to throw up." An American flight attendant commented, "It doesn't matter what airline it is– we're all in it together. It's family when it comes to this, only this time it was ours." As a companion, also an attendant, walked away to avoid a reporter, the first attendant said, "Her best friend was on that flight."

Michael Lux was returning to Phoenix with a friend when he heard the news on the car radio. "That's not my father–he flew the trip home this morning," he said. He then spoke words that would ring truer than he could have ever imagined: "But I bet I know the captain." He did, and quite well. It was his father. Unknown to him, his father had switched trips with another captain as a personal favor–Captain Lux was not originally scheduled to take Flight 191 to Los Angeles.

Coincidentally, while working as an American Airlines flight attendant early in her career, his mother also switched trips with another flight attendant just before departure as a favor (she was going to get married). The flight she was originally scheduled to work crashed in Newark, New Jersey, with no survivors.

Not at Fault

Because of their preoccupation with evaluating multiple warnings and trying to right the aircraft, the pilots never raised the landing gear. This would have reduced drag and provided some needed airspeed. Despite this, they were not faulted by either the National Transportation Safety Board (NTSB) or fellow pilots for their inability to save the flight. They simply did not have the information needed to take the action necessary to recover the aircraft. It was impossible for the captain, seated in the cockpit's left side, to see the engine/pylon's departure due to the DC-10's layout. Every pilot later put through a flight simulator programmed to recreate Flight 191's scenario "crashed." Only when they were told of the situation as it really existed were pilots able to recover – at least, in the flight simulator. And flight simulators, the technological training marvels that they are, offer no 100 percent guarantee as to what the real aircraft will do, one way or the other. Those same flight simulators had indicated that flying and landing Flight 232 (the July 19, 1989, United Airlines DC-10 that crash landed at Sioux City, Iowa) would be impossible, but it was done nonetheless.

Had the pilots any idea of the severity of their situation, they could have legally disregarded emergency procedures and lowered the nose as soon as they were clear of obstacles. That option was available to them as stated at the beginning of the Emergency Procedures section of American's operating manual for the DC-10:

> If an emergency arises for which these procedures are not adequate
> or do not apply, the crew's best judgment should prevail.

Had the engine separation occurred just seconds earlier, before V1, the takeoff would have been aborted and Flight 191 would simply have become an incident.

It will never be known what was said in the cockpit as the DC-10 rolled over and entered its dive. Were there screams of desperation or just a shocking, numbing silence? Did a crewmember leave a message to a loved one on the cockpit voice recorder (CVR) at the moment he realized that death was imminent, as had been done several times before? If so, fate and the DC-10's design saw to it that his message would never be delivered. Power was lost to the CVR as the first moments of the disaster started to unfold. As with so many other systems, the CVR received power from the number one engine. The only clues on the CVR were a "thud," followed by a word that summed everything up: "damn."

As a result of the crash, obstacle clearance became the only condition that must be met before lowering the nose to increase airspeed. The crash prompted the FAA to issue an "Emergency Order of Suspension" for the DC-10 type certificate on June 6, 1979, which effectively grounded all DC-10 aircraft for thirty-seven days. This affected eight U.S. airlines flying 134 DC-10s. The FAA went a step further on June 26, 1979, when it issued a special regulation that prohibited the "operation of any model DC-10 aircraft within the airspace of the United States." However,

The auxiliary power unit (APU), with a section of the horizontal stabilizer still attached, is lifted as two workmen steady it. A Boeing 727 can be seen taking off just above the demolished hangars, while destroyed cars can be seen in front of them.

some safety-conscious foreign airlines took action on their own. Lufthansa voluntarily grounded its fleet of DC-10s pending inspection, and Laker Airways called back two DC-10s in mid-flight and grounded its fleet of six aircraft, shutting itself down in the process as it only operated DC-10s.

Although the NTSB concluded that maintenance was to blame, the accident aircraft had not been poorly maintained. Guilty of good intentions but poor judgment, the maintenance department didn't heed McDonnell Douglas' advice, nor did they fully evaluate their amended procedure before implementing it. They could not know the tragic repercussions their actions would bring two months later. Of two DC-10 Service Bulletins issued by McDonnell Douglas pertaining to the engine mounts, maintenance elected to perform both of them, even though compliance with one of them was optional. Of forty-five Airworthiness Directives (AD) issued for the DC-10 at the time, thirty-seven of them had been complied with–the remaining eight did not apply to the aircraft involved in the crash. All six ADs applicable to the engine installation had been performed.

Luck-Good and Bad

The fire chief in charge of the crash scene told the story of a couple who lived nearest the point of impact. Their daily routine was to sleep until 3 p.m., then get up and move to the opposite end of their mobile home into the living room. Flight 191 crashed at 3:04 p.m., sending a wall of flames slamming into the end that contained the bedroom. They narrowly escaped. Flight 191 was 11 minutes late leaving the gate.

One of the two families killed in the crash was on a vacation to California. The father had been given the airline tickets as a reward for exceptional job performance.

Several people owed their lives to last minute changes. The most remarkable example was the California man who had been trying for days to reserve a seat on the flight. He was told at the standby counter just before boarding that he could have a seat but a woman pleaded for it, saying, "I have to get to Los Angeles as soon as possible." He gave her the seat. It was an act of kindness that saved his life but took hers. He took a later flight that banked over the crashed jet after takeoff, and while changing planes in Phoenix learned of his narrow escape from death. Although almost forty years have clouded his memory, he remembers her need to get to Los Angeles–to attend a funeral.

An Indiana woman who was originally booked on Flight 191 switched to a Saturday flight when her travel agent found that the fare was cheaper. She saved $11 and her life.

At least two deaths occurred as an indirect result of the disaster. A Massachusetts woman died shortly after hearing that her thirty-five-year-old son had been killed in the crash. The maintenance foreman who oversaw the engine/pylon work on the accident aircraft was shouldered with much of the blame. He couldn't handle the burden placed on him and sadly later committed suicide.

Landing gear trucks and a substantial piece of the lower fuselage await collection by investigators.

Flight 191 crashed about as close to the mobile home park as it could without killing a resident, as evidenced by this piece of the fuselage (note door opening) which landed 725 feet from the point of impact on the trailer park's easternmost street. The mobile home immediately behind the wreckage was destroyed.

Memories–Remembering and Forgetting

Captain Walter Lux was remembered with a missing man formation at his memorial service. Stearmans (a classic biplane) were used because he had just finished restoring one a week before the crash. Unfortunately, he never got a chance to fly it. Early in his aviation career he often took a twin-engine plane to altitude with a friend, cut an engine, and practiced engine-out procedures. Performed countless times, he always spoke favorite, later prophetic, words: "You never know. You never know." Unfortunately, Captain Lux did not have the luxury of altitude when he lost an engine in May 1979.

Years after the demise of Flight 191, people still visit the mobile home park or the canine training center. They tell stories about Flight 191. Others ask about the crash. The clerk at the trailer park office told of a young man who came into the office one day, about seventeen years after the crash, in a quiet and somber emotional state. He asked if she knew the location of the crash site. She did and pointed it out to him on a photo of the area that hangs on the office wall. She then pulled out an old and yellowed *Chicago Tribune* that carried stories and photos of the crash, and he sat down and quietly read them. His eyes welled with tears–as a little boy he lost his father in the crash. In his emotional state she did not ask him his name or where he came from. "I figured that he had some things to sort out in his life," she said, "and I didn't want to bother him." After he finished, he softly thanked her and left.

Once, after taking off from O'Hare airport, a man started talking about the crash to a woman seated beside him, pointing out the window to where Flight 191 went down. Her tearful response went unnoticed by the otherwise observant passenger, perhaps for the better. One can only imagine how he would have felt had he discovered that the woman sitting next to him was Lora Lux – the wife of Flight 191's captain.

One man who lost his twenty-five-year-old son built a seventy-two-acre park in a north suburb of Chicago to honor his memory. Walter Lux had a road named after him at the Embry-Riddle Aeronautical University in Prescott, Arizona.

But aside from these individual memorials, and unlike many commercial crash sites, no memorial has been erected where Flight 191 came down. Nails were tilled into the soil in an effort to deter souvenir hunters equipped with metal detectors. For a long time, nothing grew very well in the area where the plane impacted. Now grown over, the site of 273 violent deaths is just a serene field off Touhy Avenue, filled with trees and bushes. One could never imagine that an airliner had crashed there.

Five years after the crash, small reminders could still be found at the site – a torn salad dressing packet adorned with the "AA" logo, and a valve used by passengers to adjust air flow. Twenty years later, only one sign still remains. Though eventually filled in, years of settling have caused the wing impact trough to reappear as a slight depression. After heavy rains, or when the snow melts, puddles form to mark its location. But with the property for sale, it was only a matter of time before a building foundation or parking lot replaces it. Once construction was completed, the final physical reminder of the tragedy that was American Flight 191 disappeared forever.

Many would like to forget the events of May 25, 1979. Lawsuits filed against the airline, the aircraft's manufacturer and others ran into the hundreds of millions of dollars. The DC-10's already tarnished reputation worsened. A McDonnell Douglas official put it best when he said, "We're going to take a bath on this one."

Like mutilating a photograph in an effort to erase a bad memory, American changed the name on the nose of its DC-10s from "DC-10 Luxury Liner" to "American Airlines Luxury Liner," a result of the ensuing negative publicity which questioned the DC-10's safety. The revised name remained throughout the fleet's service. Not too long after the crash, American Airlines permanently retired flight number "191" in memory of the passengers and crew who perished on May 25, 1979.

More than forty years later, American Flight 191 still holds the record as the worst commercial plane crash in United States history.

But not all records were made to be broken.

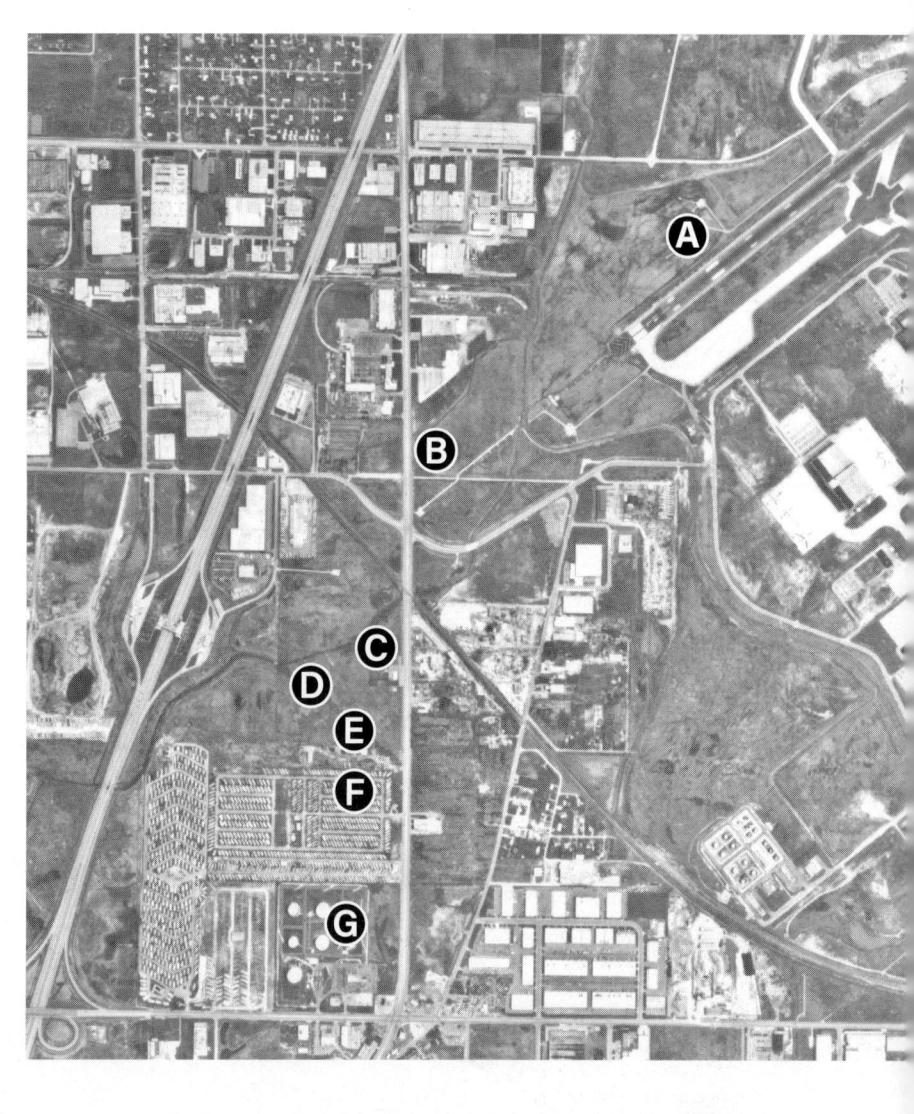

U.S. Geological Survey aerial photo taken from directly above and almost 15 years later on April 26, 1995. Note the development that has taken place compared to the previous photo. (A) Runway 32R (B) Touhy Avenue (C) Canine Training Center (D) Crash Site (E) Row of businesses destroyed by crash (F) Mobile home park (G) Fuel storage tanks.

Original photo of B-1A, serial number 74-0159, before the crash 22 miles northeast of Edwards AFB, California, on August 29, 1984, that took the life of Rockwell International chief pilot Tommie D. "Doug" Benefield. (USAF)

Chapter 16

Fuel Transfer Stalls Prototype B-1A Bomber

David L. McCurry

On August 29, 1984, Rockwell B-1A Lancer, serial number 74-0159, stalled and crashed during controllability tests at low altitude. It was the second airplane of only four prototype B-1As built for what would become the B-1B Lancer, the supersonic bomber with wings that moved forward for slow flight and back for high-speed flight. Serial number 74-0159 was on its 127th test flight, and had been modified to evaluate many of the B-1B's features designed for better flight stability and control.

The B-1A was a prototype that incorporated the F-111-type swing-wing, which provided both high- and low-altitude performance. High-altitude flight was designed at Mach 2+ and low altitude at high subsonic speeds with supersonic dash capability. The weapons load was to be greater than the B-52 for nuclear bombs, conventional bombs, and Short Range Attack Missiles (SRAMs). The B-1's range was designed to be equivalent to the B-52, but with a lower total gross weight and a much shorter takeoff roll. This would have permitted much more flexibility in basing because the B-52 is limited by its heavy gross weight and long takeoff ground roll.

B-1A 74-0159 had been scheduled to conduct a flying qualities and weapon separation flight test as part of the formal B-1 flight test program. Takeoff, weapons separation, and initial flying qualities test runs were completed without incident. It was during reconfiguration for the next test point that control of the aircraft was lost and the bomber was destroyed when it hit the ground.

The B-1 Lancer is a supersonic variable-sweep wing, heavy bomber used by the United States Air Force. It is commonly called the "Bone" in regard to its designation, "B-One." (USAF)

History of Flight

The Rockwell B-1A was engaged in minimum control speed tests at an altitude of 6,000 feet, with an F-111 flying chase. The aircraft had departed from Edwards Air Force Base, California, and was piloted by Maj. Richard V. Reynolds. In the right seat was Rockwell Chief Test Pilot Tommie D. "Doug" Benefield, and Capt. Otto J. Waniczek served as the flight test engineer.

Swinging the wings forward while over Harper Dry Lake, Maj. Reynolds neglected to properly transfer fuel in the wing tanks to adjust for the change in the center of gravity. Once the center of gravity limit was exceeded, the nose pitched upward, and the plane went into a spin at an altitude of 4,200 feet, too low for recovery.

Knowing there was nothing the crew could do to salvage the situation, Reynolds elected to use the crew escape capsule. Despite flight parameters that required the crew

The B-1A Crew Escape Module showing the left-hand Recovery Parachute repositioning trunnion still in place after the ejection and crash of 74-0159. (USAF).

to eject from the aircraft no lower than 10,000 feet, Reynolds and Benefield delayed the decision to eject and continued efforts to recover the aircraft. Separation occurred satisfactorily 1,500 feet above the ground, but a malfunction of one of the explosive repositioning bolts caused the parachutes to deploy improperly. Because of the malfunctioning mechanism, the parachutes didn't reposition to allow the escape capsule to touch down softly on its inflatable landing bag. Instead, the module struck the ground at a steep nose-down angle, hurtling the crew forward into the control panels.

The capsule landed about 200 feet from the main impact point. When the capsule struck the ground, Reynolds sustained serious back injuries, Benefield died when his seat ripped away from the floor of the capsule due to the 40g impact forces, and Waniczek, who was not wearing his helmet or harness, also suffered serious injuries.

The bomber came down tail-first with about 90,000 pounds of fuel aboard. The plane crashed and burned northwest of Harper Dry Lake, California, some twenty-two miles northeast of Edwards and about nine miles northeast of Kramer Junction. Emergency crews from Edwards soon arrived and sealed off the site.

This was the first operational use of the escape system that was only installed on the first three B-1A prototypes. After this incident, the B-1 crew escape capsule system was abandoned. The fourth B-1A and production B-1B bombers were equipped with individual ejection seats for all crewmembers.

Our wreck hunting group discovering larger pieces of the crashed B-1A bomber. After the investigation was completed, the entire site was bulldozed leaving some wreckage buried. (Dave McCurry)

Conclusions

One lesson learned from this accident was the importance of crew composition. In this case, the least experienced pilot was assigned as aircraft commander with the most experienced crewmember as copilot. This inequity impacted efficient cockpit resource management. In addition, it was a common occurrence during the test missions for the center-of-gravity warning light to flash. It did so often enough that ignoring it had become routine; a situation described as "warning light fatigue." In retrospect, that highlighted another area of concern that was communication. The center-of gravity issues appeared frequently, but the crew didn't discuss them and failed to properly interpret what the aircraft was trying to communicate.

Small fragments of burned aluminum as seen at the crash site of the B-1A Lancer bomber aircraft. (Dave McCurry)

Not all of the problems had originated in the cockpit. For this flight, a less experienced mission planner had arranged the test-point sequence. Organization of flight objectives is important in carrying out a mission and additionally, between two test points, flight controllers left their mission control stations for a brief meeting. This left no one to monitor the center-of-gravity values on telemetry monitors and so another opportunity to warn the crew was lost. Following the crash of the B-1A, control room procedure changes were implemented to prevent a similar accident in the future.

The Crash Site Today

After the investigation and initial cleanup, the crash site was bulldozed leaving very little debris at the site. Interestingly the ground at the crash site is almost completely void of vegetation probably due to jet fuel contamination.

The site appears as a large white spot from a distance out on the open desert. On closer inspection, the entire crash site is covered with small fragments of burned twisted aluminum. We found a few parts with inspection stamps, part numbers, and dates, but nothing that was immediately identifiable. Some of the small parts seen were painted with a white "anti-glare" type paint.

There is a very nice memorial at the site which includes a plate-steel silhouette of the B-1 bomber, an American flag, and a small rock cairn containing a flag and short story about Tommie D. "Doug" Benefield. Historically, the Edwards Air Force Base and Mojave Marine Corps Axillary Air Station areas were intense testing and training sites, and contain hundreds of crash sites within a fifty-mile radius.

Today, a nice memorial marker (a welded plate-steel silhouette of the crashed B-1A bomber) is placed at the crash site along with a steel plate bearing the name of Tommie D. Benefield. (Dave McCurry)

Bibliography and Suggested Reading

Alexander, Sigmund Col. *B-47 Aircraft Losses.* Spiral bound and available direct from the author (12110 Los Cerdos St., San Antonio, TX 78233-5953); Newspaper clippings, reports, and photos of all B-47 losses. http://www.b-47.com/SAC%20Accidents.htm

Andrade, John M. *U.S. Military Aircraft Designations and Serials Since 1909.* Hinckley, Leics, Endland. Midland Counties Publications, 1979.

Badcock, Capt. T.C. *A Broken Arrow: The Story of the Arrow Air Disaster in Gander, Newfoundland.* St. John's, Newfoundland. Al Clouston Publications. 1988.

Bailey, Dan E. *World War II Wrecks of the Truk Lagoon.* Redding, California. North Valley Diver Publications. 2000.

_____. *WWII Wrecks of the Kwajalein and Truk Lagoons.* Redding, California. North Valley Diver Publications. 1989.

_____. *World War II Wrecks of Palau.* Redding, California. North Valley Diver Publications. 1991.

Bartelski, Jan. *Disasters in the Air: Mysterious Air Disasters Explained.* London. Airlife Publishing, Ltd. 2001.

Bradley, E. Philip with Richard F. Gaya Sr. *The Crash of Piedmont Flight 349 into Bucks Elbow Mt. as told by the Sole Survivor, E. Philip Bradley.* Available direct from the author: Philip Bradley, P.O. Box 3219, Monroe, NC 28111-3219

Brandt, Trey. *Faded Contrails: Last Flights Over Arizona.* Phoenix, Ariz. Acacia Publishers, 2003.

Burtness, Robert A. *The Santa Barbara B-24 Disasters: A Chain of Tragedies Across Air, Land & Sea.* Charleston, South Carolina. 2012.

Cass, William F. The Last Flight of Liberator 41-1133: *The Lives, Times, Training and the Loss of the Bomber Crew Which Crashed on Trail Peak at Philmont Scout Ranch.* West Chester, Pennsylvania. The Winds Aloft Press. 1996.

Childers, Thomas. *Wings of Morning: The Story of the Last American Bomber Shot Down Over Germany in World War II.* Reading, Mass. Addison-Wesley Publishing Co. 1995.

Cole, Ben. *Four Down on Old Peachtree Road.* Suwanee, Georgia. Crosswind Publications, Ltd. 2007.

Collier, Ron and Ron Wilkinson. *Dark Peak Wrecks* (Vols. 1 and 2). London, England. Pen & Sword Books. 1997.

Copas, Jerry. *The Wreck of the Naval Airship USS* Shenandoah. Charleston, South Carolina. Arcadia Publishing. 2017.

Corsetti III, Emilio. *35 Miles from Shore: The Ditching and Rescue of ALM Flight 980.* Lake St. Louis, Missouri. Odyssey Publishing LLC. 2008.

Darby, Charles. *Pacific Aircraft Wrecks…And Where to Find Them.* Melbourne, Australia. Kookaburra Technical Publications Party Ltd., 1979.

Denham, Terry. *World Directory of Airliner Crashes: A Comprehensive Record of more than 10,000 Passenger Aircraft Accidents.* Somerset, England. Patrick Stephens Ltd., 1996.

Doylerush, Edward. *Rocks in the Clouds: High-Ground Aircraft Crashes of South Wales.* Hersham, Surry, England. Midland Publishing/Ian Allan Publishing Ltd. 2008.

Faith, Nicholas. *Black Box: Why Air Safety Is No Accident.* Osceola, Wisc. MBI Publishing. 1996.

Field, Andrew J. Mainliner *Denver: The Bombing of Flight 629.* Boulder, Colorado. Johnson Books. 2005.

Fortenberry, Ken H. *Flight 7 is Missing: The Search for My Father's Killer.* Columbus, Ohio. Fayetteville Mafia Press. 2020.

Hayes, David. *The Lost Squadron: A Fleet of Warplanes Locked in Ice for 50 Years…Can They be Freed to Fly Again?* New York. Hyperion. 1994.

Heitman, *William P. Music's Broken Wings: Fifty Years of Aviation Accidents in the Music Industry.* Durham, North Carolina. Dreamflyer Publications. 2003.

Hersh, Seymour M. *The Target is Destroyed: What Really Happened to Flight 007 And What America Knew About It.* New York. Random House. 1986.

Hoffman, Carl. *Hunting Warbirds: The Obsessive Quest for the Lost Aircraft of World War II.* New York. Ballantine Books. 2001.

Imparato, Edward T. *Into Darkness: A Pilot's Journey Through Headhunter Territory.* Charlottesville, Virginia. Howell Press, Inc. 1995.

Job, Macarthur. *Air Disaster.* Weston Creek, Australia. Aerospace Publications Pty. Ltd. 1994. Volumes One through Four (published in 1995, 1996, 1999, and 2001 respectively).

Johnston, Moira. *The Last Nine Minutes: The Story of Flight 981.* New York. William Morrow and Co., Inc. 1976.

Kearns, David A. *Where Hell Freezes Over: A Story of Amazing Bravery and Survival.* New York. Thomas Dunne Books (St. Martin's Press). 2005.

Lee, Robert Mason. *Death and Deliverance: The True Story of an Airplane Crash at the North Pole.* Golden, Colo. Fulcrum Publishing. 1993.

Leifer, Gregory P. *Aviation Mysteries of the North: Disappearances in Alaska and Canada.* Anchorage, Alaska. Publication Consultants. 2011.

Lyssenko, Taras. C. *The Great Navy Birds of Lake Michigan: The True Story of the Privateers of Lake Michigan and the Aircraft They Rescued.* Charleston, South Carolina. America Through Time. 2019.

McClendon, Dennis E. *The Lady Be Good: Mystery Bomber of World War II.* Fallbrook, Calif. Aero Publishers. 1962.

McGregor, Kevin A. *Flight of Gold: Two Pilots' True Adventure Discovering Alaska's Legendary Gold Wreck.* Holland, Michigan. In-Depth Editions. 2013.

McLachlan, Ian. Final Flights, *Dramatic Wartime Incidents Revealed by Aviation Archaeology.* Haynes Publishing. London. 1995.

Macha, Gary Patric and Don Jordan. *Aircraft Wrecks in the Mountains and Deserts of California* (1909-2002, Third Edition). Lake Forest, CA. InfoNet Publishing, 2002.

Macha, G. Pat. *Historic Aircraft Wrecks of Los Angeles County.* Charleston, South Carolina. The History Press. 2014.
_____. *Historic Aircraft Wrecks of San Bernardino County.* Charleston, South Carolina. The History Press. 2013
_____. *Historic Aircraft Wrecks of San Diego County.* Charleston, South Carolina. The History Press. 2016

McCurry, David L., Cye Laramie, and Dan Thomas Nelson. *Aircraft Wrecks of the Pacific Northwest.* Bennington, Vermont. Merriam Press Military History. 2013.

McCurry, David L., Don Hinton, and Cye Laramie. *Aircraft Wrecks of the Pacific Northwest. Vol. 2.* Bennington, Vermont. Merriam Press Military History. 2014.

McCurry, David L. with Cye Laramie. *Aircraft Wrecks of the Pacific Northwest. Vol. 3.* Hoosick Falls, New York. Merriam Press Military History. 2017.

McCurry, David L. *Aircraft Wrecks of the Western States: Vol. 1.* Hoosick Falls, New York. Merriam Press, 2020.

McCurry, David L., Don Hinton, et. al. *Aircraft Wrecks of the Western States: Vol. 2.* Lulu.com, 2021.

Mann, Robert A. *Aircraft Record Cards of the United States Air Force (How to Read the Codes).* Jefferson, North Carolina. McFarland & Co. Publishers, 2008.

Martinez, Mario. *Lady's Men: The Story of World War II's Mystery Bomber and her Crew.* Annapolis, Md. Naval Institute Press. 1995.

Matzen, Robert. *Fireball: Carole Lombard and the Mystery of Flight 3.* Pittsburgh, Pennsylvania. GoodKnight Books. 2014.

Merlin, Peter W. and Tony Moore. *X-Plane Crashes: Exploring Experimental, Rocket Plane, and Spycraft Incidents, Accidents and Crash Sites.* North Branch, Minnesota. Specialty Press, 2008.

Mireles, Anthony J. *Fatal Army Air Forces Aviation Accidents in the United States, 1941-1945* (three volumes). Jefferson, North Carolina. McFarland & Co. Publishers, 2006.

Morrison, Lee. B. *Out of the Wilderness: Restoring a Relic.* North Canton, Ohio. Military Aviation Preservation Society. 1995.

Page, Gordon. Warbird Recovery: *The Hunt for a Rare WWII Plane in Siberia, Russia.* New York. iUniverse. 2005.

Panas, Jr., John. *Aircraft Mishap Photography: Documenting the Evidence.* Ames, Iowa. Iowa State University Press. 1996.

Plaskon, Kyril D. *Silent Heroes of the Cold War: The Mysterious Military Plane Crash on a Nevada Mountain Peak and the Families Who Endured an Abyss of Silence for Generations.* Las Vegas, Nevada. Stephens Press LLC. 2009.

Quinn, Chuck Marrs. *The Aluminum Trail: China, Burma, India, World War II, 1942-1945.* Self-published. 1989.

Ralph, Barry. *The Crash of Little Eva: The Ultimate World War II Survivor Story.* Gretna, Louisiana. Pelican Publishing Co. 2004.

Septer, Dirk. *Lost Nuke: The Last Flight of Bomber 075.* Victoria, Canada. Heritage House Publishing. 2012.

Serling, Robert J. *The Probable Cause…The Truth About Air Travel Today.* Garden City, New York. Doubleday & Co. 1960.

Shaw, Adam. *Sound of Impact: The Legacy of TWA Flight 514.* New York. The Viking Press. 1977.

Sheehan, Susan. *A Missing Plane.* New York. G.P. Putnam's Sons. 1986.

Smith, David J. *High Ground Wrecks and Relics: Aircraft Hulks on the Mountains of the UK and Ireland.* Leicester, England. Midland Publishing Ltd. 1997.

Starks, Richard and Miriam Murcutt. *Lost in Tibet: The Untold Story of Five American Airmen, a Doomed Plane, and the Will to Survive.* Guilford, Connecticut. The Lyons Press. 2004.

Stekel, Peter. *Final Flight: The Mystery of a WWII Plane Crash and the Frozen Airmen in the High Sierra.* Berkeley, California. Wilderness Press. 2010.
_____. *Beneath Haunted Waters: The Tragic Tale of Two B-24s Lost in the Sierra Nevada Mountains during World War II.* Guilford, Connecticut. Lyons Press. 2017.

Sterling, Bryan B. and Frances N. Sterling. *Will Rogers & Wiley Post: Death At Barrow.* New York. M. Evans and Co. 1993.

Stewart, Stanley. Emergency! *Crisis in The Cockpit.* New York. Tab Books/McGraw Hill. 1989

Sturkey, Marion. *Mid-Air: Accident Reports and Voice Transcripts from Military and Airline Mid-Air Collisions.* Plum Branch, South Carolina. Heritage Press International. 2008.

Van Waarde, Jan. *US Military Aircraft Mishaps 1950-2004.* Schipol, The Netherlands. Scramble/Dutch Aviation Society. 2005.

Veronico, Nicholas A. *Hidden Warbirds: The Epic Stories of Finding, Recovering, and Restoring Lost Aircraft.* Zenith Press. Minneapolis, Minnesota. 2013.
_____. *Hidden Warbirds II: More Epic Stories of Finding, Recovering, Restoring Lost Aircraft.* Zenith Press. Minneapolis, Minnesota. 2014.

Veronico, Nicholas A., Ed Davies, et. al. *Wreckchasing: A Guide to Finding Aircraft Crash Sites.* Castro Valley, CA; Pacific Aero Press, 1992.

Veronico, Nicholas A., Ed Davies, Donald B. McComb Jr., and Michael B. McComb. *Wreckchasing 2: Commercial Aircraft Crashes and Crash Sites.* Miami, FL. World Transport Press, 1996.

Veronico, Nicholas A., Ed Davies, A. Kevin Grantham, Robert A. Kropp, Enrico Massagli, Donald B. McComb Jr., Michael B. McComb, Thomas Wm. McGarry, Walt Wentz. *Wreckchasing 101: A Guide to Finding Aircraft Crash Sites.* Minneapolis, Minnesota. Stance and Speed. 2011.

Ward, Chris and Andreas Wachtel. *Dambuster Crash Sites: 617 Dambuster Squadron Crash Sites in Holland & Germany.* Pen & Sword Books, England. 2007

Weisheit, Bowen P. *The Last Flight of Ensign C. Markland Kelly, Junior, USNR: Battle of Midway, June 4, 1942.* The Ensign C. Markland Kelly, Jr., Memorial Foundation, Inc. Baltimore, Maryland. 1993.

Wetterhahn, Ralph F. *Last Flight of Bomber 31.* New York. Garroll & Graf Publishers. 2004.

Whitby, Steven R. *No Way Out: The Untold Story of the B-24 Lady Be Good and Her Crews.* Atglen, Pennsylvania. Schiffer Military History. 2020.

Widner, Robert. *Aircraft Accidents in Florida: From Pearl Harbor to Hiroshima.* Lulu.com. 2009.

Williams, Charles M. *The Crash of TWA Flight 260.* Albuquerque, New Mexico. University of New Mexico Press. 2010.

Young, Cindy Lou. *Out of the Fog: Tragedy on Nantucket.* Alton, New Hampshire. Black Lab Publishing, LLC. 2008.

Some photo chronicles and other resource books that should be on your shelves:

Davis, Larry. *Bent & Battered Wings: USAAF/USAF Damaged Aircraft, 1935-1957* (Vol. 2). Carrollton, Texas. Squadron/Signal Publications Inc. 1989.

Gallagher, James P. Meatballs and Dead Birds: *A Photo Gallery of Destroyed Japanese Aircraft in World War II*. Mechanicsburg, Pennsylvania, 2004.

Graff, Cory. *Shot to Hell: The Stories and Photos of Ravaged WWII Warbirds*. St. Paul, Minnesota. MBI Publishing Co. 2003.
_____. *Clear the Deck! Aircraft Carrier Accidents of World War II*. North Branch, Minnesota. Specialty Press. 2008.

Grantham, A. Kevin. *P-Screamers: The History of the Surviving Lockheed P-38 Lightnings*. Missoula, Montana. Pictorial Histories Publishing Co. Inc. 1994.

Green, Brett. Götterdämmerung: *Luftwaffe Wrecks and Relics*. London. Classic/Ian Allan Publishing. 2006.

Kenney, Douglas and William Butler. *No Easy Days: The Incredible Drama of Naval Aviation*. Louisville, Ky. Avion Park Publishing. 1995.

Mikesh, Robert C. Broken *Wings of the Samurai: The Destruction of the Japanese Airforce*. Annapolis, Maryland. Naval Institute Press. 1993.

Sullivan, Jim. *Bent & Battered Wings: USN/USMC Damaged Aircraft, 1943-1953*. Carrollton, Texas. Squadron/Signal Publications Inc. 1986.

Thompson, Scott A. *B-25 Mitchell in Civil Service. Aero Vintage Books.* Elk Grove, Calif. 1997.
_____. *Final Cut: The Post-War B-17 Flying Fortress and Survivors* (Third Edition). Pictorial Histories Publishing. Missoula, Mont. 2009.

About the Authors

Ian E. Abbott
Ian Abbott has been interested in aviation since childhood. He visited his first wreck site, that of a U.S. Navy F2H-4 Banshee, in 1993. Following that experience, he has visited a wide variety of military and civilian wreck sites, mostly within California. His interest in early radio and navigation equipment has helped him identify the remains of components and vacuum tubes he has found at many wrecks. He earned a bachelor's degree in Aviation (Operations) at San Jose State University, as well as an FAA mechanic certificate with Airframe and Powerplant ratings. His other interests include photography and amateur radio.

Jeff Christner
Jeff Christner and his son Paxton started Wreckchasing as a father-son activity in 2007. Starting out by visiting known crash site locations, Jeff soon began researching other crash sites which had not been previously located by other Wreckchasers. Since then, they have researched and located over half a dozen crash sites whose exact locations had been lost to history once the investigation into the crash was complete and the site cleaned up. They have also assisted other members of the Wreckchasing community by helping perform crash site surveys due to their expertise in the use of metal detectors.

Ed Davies
Born in Wales, England, Ed Davies graduated as an electrical engineer and completed two years full time national service as a sub lieutenant in the Fleet Air Arm of the Royal Navy. He worked as an engineer in a nuclear power plant before emigrating to North America in 1966. Davies held various managerial positions in the aluminum industry before branching out in his own business in 1983. He retired to devote more time to his hobby of aviation research in general, and the history of surviving DC-3s in particular. He has written many articles for the aviation press in the U.K. and the United States and has co-authored *Wreckchasing 101: A Guide to Finding Aircraft Crash Sites* and *Douglas DC-3: 60 Years and Counting*.

Craig Fuller
Craig Fuller has researched and documented over 1,000 aircraft crash sites throughout the United States, Europe, and Micronesia. He was formerly the chief flight instructor at Arizona State University and has more than 3,000 hours of flight experience. In 1997, he formed AAIR, Aviation Archaeological Investigation and Research (www.AviationArchaeology.com), a business dedicated to researching and documenting old aircraft crashes and providing historic documents, including accident reports. Fuller holds a Bachelor of Science degree in Aeronautical Science with a minor in Aviation Safety-Accident Investigation from Embry Riddle Aeronautical University, and studied archaeology at Sonoma State University.

David L. McCurry
Author David L. McCurry grew up in the Pacific Northwest and spent the majority of his life serving as a professional pilot doing charter flying, flight instructing, and contract flying. During his 50-plus year career, he has had the opportunity to fly more than 200 types of single and multi-engine aircraft. McCurry has always had a strong interest in aviation history and has spent the past 25 years studying old and rare aircraft crash sites located throughout the western United States. From that research, he has authored five books titled *Aircraft Wrecks of the Pacific Northwest*, and *Aircraft Wrecks of the Western States*. Other interests include travelling to destinations all over the globe, hiking, and photo work.

Michael H. Marlow
Mike Marlow has been a life-long aviation enthusiast, specializing in commercial aircraft and airlines of the Deregulation-era. Having a career in high-tech has afforded him the opportunity to travel to a wide variety of historic aircraft crash sites on both coasts. He has a particular interest in the root causes and chains of events that have led to commercial flights terminating in crashes. On the opposite side of the interest spectrum, he has a passion for dramatic fiction stories, and is currently developing a number of projects for print and movies.

Tony Moore
Tony Moore was fascinated with the idea of Wreckchasing as a child after seeing photos of the XB-70 crash site in the Mojave Desert. Many years later, together with Peter Merlin, they would form The X-Hunters Aerospace Archeology Team and visit not only the XB-70, but many other legendary aircraft sites scattered across the Southwest. Training as an FAA certified Airframe and Powerplant mechanic would come in useful to help positively identify some of the aircraft and artifacts located at these sites. Tony has also served as the Film and Video Archivist at the NASA Dryden (Armstrong) Flight Research Center and as the Museum Specialist/Curator for the Air Force Flight Test Museum at Edward's Air Force Base. In 2007, together with Peter Merlin, he wrote, *X-Plane Crashes: Exploring Experimental, Rocket Plane, and Spy Craft Incidents, Accidents, and Crash Sites*.

James Douglas Scroggins III
Doug Scroggins first visited an aircraft wreck site in 1985, and soon began to visit hundreds of other sites in the western United States. Operating a film/video production company, he documented these sites, producing a video and publishing a magazine, *Lost Birds*. His aviation career expanded and he opened Scroggins Aviation, a company that specialized in commercial aircraft dismantling, crash recovery, recycling, and parts sales. He went on to produce a TV documentary *Scrapping Aircraft Giants* and co-authored the book *Junkyard Jets*, about the end of live process of commercial jet aircraft. He then restructured his business and now operates Scroggins Aviation Mockup & Effects, a company that supplies airplanes and helicopters to the film and television industry. Some of the films the company has supplied mock-ups for include *Flight*, *Jurassic World*, *Sully*, *Spider-Man: Homecoming*, *Dunkirk*, *Deadpool 2*, and *Plane*, to name a few.

Scott Thompson 
Scott Thompson is an aviation historian and photographer who has written numerous books and articles about vintage aircraft and warbirds. His primary historical interest has concentrated on the postwar use of the B-17, and maintains a website at aerovintage.com. He has also specialized in documenting the history of Hollywood pilots Paul Mantz and Frank Tallman, and maintains another website at tallmantz.com. He retired from a long career as an FAA flight inspection pilot in November 2021, and lives with his wife in Lincoln, California. He is the author of *Final Cut: The Post-War B-17 Flying Fortress and Survivors, B-17 in Blue: The Flying Fortress in U.S. Navy and Coast Guard Service*, as well as *B-25 Mitchell in Civil Service*.

David Trojan 
David Trojan is a Navy veteran who served 21 years as an Aviation Electronics Technician retiring in 2000. After retiring he became an Aircraft Engineer for the Marine Corps. Trojan has investigated and visited more than 500 military aircraft crash sites all across the country and the world. He has written over 80 published articles for numerous local newspapers and aviation magazines, including *Naval Aviation, WWI Aero*, and *Warbirds International*. He has been featured on the Armed Forces TV network, podcasts and YouTube.

Trojan likes to discover the facts, fill in the blanks, explain the mysteries of why the planes crashed and finally lay the questions to rest by speaking and writing about their stories. The stories give light to those who have sacrificed so much to give us the peace we enjoy today.

Nicholas A. Veronico 
Nicholas A. Veronico has had an interesting career in aviation having worked for a number of leading publications, and he spent the last 25 years as a contractor working at NASA on various projects. Veronico's last assignment was leading the communications effort for the prime contractor operating NASA's Stratospheric Observatory for Infrared Astronomy (SOFIA) – a highly modified Boeing 747SP fitted with a 2.7-meter telescope. He has written more than 45 books, including the *Hidden Warbirds* series as well as *Hidden Warships*, and is a co-author of the *Wreckchasing* series. In 1995, he started www.wreckchasing.com – an online community for enthusiasts interested in locating, documenting, and preserving historic aircraft wrecks. He hosted the first symposium for those interested in aviation archaeology and wreckchasing in 2009.